THE SMART APPROACH TO
KITCHEN DESIGN

THE SMART APPROACH TO
KITCHEN DESIGN

Susan Maney

CREATIVE HOMEOWNER®, Upper Saddle River, New Jersey

Editorial Director: Timothy O. Bakke
Art Director: W. David Houser

Editor: Kathie Robitz
Associate Editor: Lynn Elliott
Copy Editor: Louise I. Driben
Indexer: Sandi Schroeder

Design and Layout: Monduane Harris
Illustrator: Vincent Alessi

Cover Design: Annie Jeon
Cover Photography: Nancy Hill

Printed in the United States of America

Current Printing (last digit)
10 9 8

The Smart Approach To Kitchen Design, First Edition
Library of Congress Catalog Card Number: 98-84953
ISBN: 1-58011-024-X

CREATIVE HOMEOWNER®
A Division of Federal Marketing Corp.
24 Park Way
Upper Saddle River, NJ 07458
Web site: **www.creativehomeowner.com**

DEDICATION

I dedicate this book to my best friend, Juleen Peacock, who turned my kitchen into a work of art.

ACKNOWLEDGMENTS

I want to thank everyone who shared their ideas and experience for this book. I especially want to thank my family and friends for their encouragement and support. A special thanks goes to my editor, Kathie Robitz, who has touched me with her kindness and hard work.

CONTENTS

INTRODUCTION

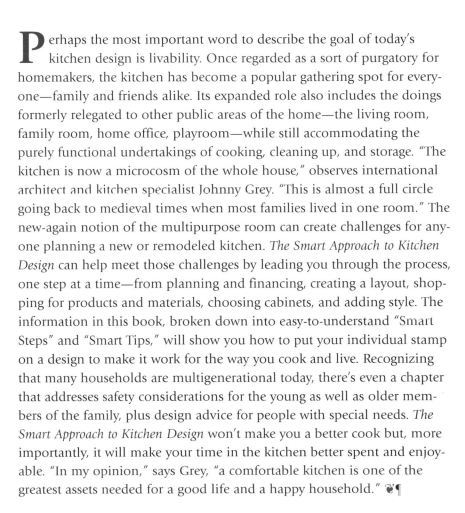

Perhaps the most important word to describe the goal of today's kitchen design is livability. Once regarded as a sort of purgatory for homemakers, the kitchen has become a popular gathering spot for everyone—family and friends alike. Its expanded role also includes the doings formerly relegated to other public areas of the home—the living room, family room, home office, playroom—while still accommodating the purely functional undertakings of cooking, cleaning up, and storage. "The kitchen is now a microcosm of the whole house," observes international architect and kitchen specialist Johnny Grey. "This is almost a full circle going back to medieval times when most families lived in one room." The new-again notion of the multipurpose room can create challenges for anyone planning a new or remodeled kitchen. *The Smart Approach to Kitchen Design* can help meet those challenges by leading you through the process, one step at a time—from planning and financing, creating a layout, shopping for products and materials, choosing cabinets, and adding style. The information in this book, broken down into easy-to-understand "Smart Steps" and "Smart Tips," will show you how to put your individual stamp on a design to make it work for the way you cook and live. Recognizing that many households are multigenerational today, there's even a chapter that addresses safety considerations for the young as well as older members of the family, plus design advice for people with special needs. *The Smart Approach to Kitchen Design* won't make you a better cook but, more importantly, it will make your time in the kitchen better spent and enjoyable. "In my opinion," says Grey, "a comfortable kitchen is one of the greatest assets needed for a good life and a happy household." ❦¶

Opposite and left, top to bottom: *"The kitchen is not just a refueling station," says designer Johnny Grey, "it's [also] a place to live in, relax, and be sociable." This Grey-designed space features his trademark "unfitted look," of stand-alone pieces for storage and work space that resemble highly individualistic furnishings.*

THE BIG PICTURE

The photographs in this book will provide lots of inspiration for your new kitchen. Visions of gastronomical feats or even modest microwaveable meals may dance in your head, but the road to an efficient plan will be full of important decisions about who will actually do the work and what it will cost. After all, the space you want to create may very well cater not only to you and your family's cooking and dining habits, but may also provide a place for you to pay the bills, the children to do their homework, or the entire family to indulge in hobbies. It's fine to window-shop, comb through books and magazines filled with appealing pictures, and make lists of all the things you want your new kitchen to be, and doing these things should be part of your homework, but you're eventually going to have to come down to earth and take stock of the big picture. Ultimately, your careful analysis and planning is what can make or break the successful outcome of your endeavors.

The kitchen is truly the heart of the home. While committing to a remodeling project of this size can be intimidating and exciting at the same time, you shouldn't allow either your enthusiasm or concerns to cloud your way. To remain objective and keep from feeling overwhelmed, don't think about everything at once. Take it easy, slow down, do your research. Once you have done all of this, then and only then are you ready to consider all of the options regarding who will be involved in all aspects of the work and how you will pay for it.

Left: *Today's kitchen is the real living room in most homes. Often, it requires a team of professionals to create a design that is personal, livable, and efficient. Here, a large subdivided layout contains a media room at one end and a dining area at the other. The kitchen's work zone, in the center, anchors the space.*

SMART STEPS

ONE: *Get the right help.* Redesigning and remodeling a kitchen requires skill and knowledge. It is the most difficult room in the house to remodel and the most costly—not a project most do-it-yourselfers will feel comfortable tackling alone. In most cases, you will need to seek professional help at some point, depending on your particular level of skill. But who should you use? There are many different kinds of professionals who can assist you. Here is a short list of those who would be qualified to offer advice.

Right and below: *In the dining area, a built-in banquette comfortably seats six people without taking up lots of floor space. The designer used mirrors to visually expand the space. Built-in cabinets in the media room hold the TV and sound equipment.*

Opposite: *A custom-designed cooking center artfully houses the professional-style range and adjacent ovens. It gives the appearances of a large hearth—a throwback to the time when the kitchen fireplace was the heart of the home.*

❦ **Architects.** If you are planning a significant structural change in your kitchen, an architect is your best choice. Be sure to find one who specializes in residential design. However, the *possible* exception, if you are a very serious cook who often prepares meals for large groups, is a commercial architect who specializes in restaurant planning and would be willing to work on a small project. There are significant differences between residential and commercial design techniques. Although all architects are schooled to design both environments, someone who regularly designs kitchens for a family rather than an entire army or boardinghouse is better-suited for your purpose. The letters AIA after an architect's name indicate membership in the American Institute of Architects, a national association with local and state chapters that readily offer referral services.

❦ **Certified Kitchen Designers.** Called CKDs, these people are trained and certified specifically in kitchen design and remodeling by the National Kitchen and Bath Association (NKBA). Because they are specialists, they know the latest in kitchen products and trends, and are highly qualified to devise the best layout and help you choose the most appropriate materials and appliances for your particular project.

Left: *The designer of this California kitchen used earthy materials and colors to ease the transition from inside to outdoors.*

Opposite: *On the East Coast, another designer used traditional forms to create a formal look in this kitchen.*

something goes wrong, you only have to make one call. There is no passing the buck here: one boss, one client.

❧ **Remodeling Contractors.** Some contractors offer design help as part of their remodeling services or they are in partnership with a design professional. Contractors are good choices if you have already hired an architect to design the kitchen or if you are not making substantial structural changes to the room. One good example of when to choose a remodeling contractor is when you are simply refacing cabinets or reconfiguring the existing space for more efficiency in your kitchen layout.

Whenever you hire people to work in your house, take the time to research them carefully. Your home is likely your largest single asset; don't take chances with it unnecessarily. Interview professionals, inspect their portfolios, ask them for references and, by all means, follow up by checking their references thoroughly. Ask tough questions both of them and their former clients. It's also wise to call state agencies and trade associations to inquire about the credentials of anyone you engage for the project.

❧ **Interior Designers.** Interior designers can help you create and integrate style in your kitchen and throughout your home. They do not make structural changes, but work with color, pattern, texture, and furnishings to shape a design. You may want to contact an interior designer if you are making significant cosmetic changes to your kitchen. The letters ASID after an interior designer's name indicates membership in the American Society of Interior Designers, a national organization. For members to use "ASID" after their name, they must pass the National Council for Interior Design Qualification exam. Local or state chapters of the ASID can provide member referrals. Some states require licensing.

❧ **Design-Build Remodeling Firms.** These firms offer one-stop shopping for design services and construction provided by designers and remodelers who are on staff. If

TWO: *Establish a working budget.* This is the not-so-fun part—finding and parting with money. No one likes to crunch numbers, but establishing a budget is the only way to determine the size and scope of your project. It is very disappointing to plan a state-of-the-art kitchen that could rival any well-known chef's only to find you can barely afford a new cooktop and fresh wallpaper. Don't shy away from big dreams, just don't get your heart set on any luxury until you determine what you can honestly afford to spend on the project.

Try to avoid paying cash for remodeling. If it comes down to a choice between paying cash for a new kitchen or for buying a car, always finance the remodeling. You can deduct the interest of the remodeling loan from your taxes; you can't deduct the interest on a car loan. Unfortunately, many homeowners will gladly use cash to pay for a home-improvement project and take out a loan for a car. It just doesn't make sense.

Remember that whomever you choose to remodel your kitchen will end up knowing you and your family better than your lawyer or doctor. He or she will see you first thing in the morning and will probably still be there when you come home after a long work day. So, scrutinize all professionals out as closely as you would prospective tenants.

In addition to obtaining professional help, you will want to get first-hand advice from friends who have already been through the kitchen remodeling process. No one source will be able to answer every question or meet every need, but the best approach is education. Clip out photographs in magazines for visual ideas, collect notes and ideas, and hit the Internet and home shows on TV for further inspiration and handy tips that may save you time or money.

Take all these bits of information and put them in one place—a dream book, a looseleaf binder, a drawer, or even an idea box. This is the fun part of remodeling. It is the time for fantasizing and making wish lists of all those design elements you have coveted for years—until your feet hit the ground and you wake up to the reality of *money*.

Smart Tip about References

Ask professionals for as many references as possible, but get at least three. When you speak to former clients, don't limit your questions to, "Did John Smith and his company do a good job?" You should be more detailed. Here are a few of the top questions to ask, as recommended by the National Association of the Remodeling Industry (NARI):

- Could you communicate well with the remodeler?
- Were you satisfied with the remodeler's business practices?
- Did the crew show up on time?
- Were you comfortable with the tradespeople the remodeler contracted?
- Was the job completed on schedule? On budget?
- Did the remodeler fulfill his or her contract?
- Did the remodeler stay in touch throughout the project?
- Would you use the remodeler again without hesitation?

Smart Tip about Financing

Any bank or lending institution will be happy to tell you how much you can afford to spend on your home-remodeling project. But if you feel more comfortable running a test on your own, here is a quick and easy-to-understand overview of how banks figure out what you can spend.

The debt-to-income (DTI) ratio

This tells a lender if you can handle more debt on your current level of income. While each lender will have its own approved DTI, the average is normally at least 45 percent.

Current monthly expenses $_____

Add the estimated monthly

   remodeling payment   +_____

Total expenses $_____

Divide by your gross monthly income   ÷_____

This is your DTI   _____%

How to find your maximum payment for remodeling

If your DTI doesn't qualify for financing options, you may need to lower the monthly remodeling expenditure. This calculation will show you how low you need to go.

Gross monthly income $_____

Multiply by lender's DTI ratio   ×_____

Subtotal $_____

Subtract your total monthly expenses

(not counting the estimated remodeling payment)   −_____

This gives you your maximum payment of $_____

If the last line is negative, you may have to scale back your plans or do the work yourself on a very tight budget. A negative number means you won't be receiving funds from a lender. On the other hand, you could check out other funding options. For example, consider a consolidation loan, which allows you to incorporate your current debts into the home-improvement loan. A consolidation loan does two things for you. First, it lowers the monthly cost of your current debts. Second, it allows you to deduct the interest on the loan from your taxes, something you can't do on other forms of debt.

You might also think about other forms of financing besides home equity loans. There are a variety of them in today's financial market. You could take out a loan against investments, borrow against your credit card, or the perennial favorite: Obtain a private loan from a family member.

THREE: *Familiarize yourself with legal issues.* Anytime you enter into an agreement you are venturing into the legal world of a litigious society. As one of the contractual parties, you do have certain rights. For example, you can change your mind. This is called the "Right of Recision," which allows you to change your mind within three days of

Left: *High-ticket items such as custom cabinetry, hardwood floors, and exquisite tile decorated with a hand-painted* toile de Jouy *pattern can triple the cost of a standard kitchen remodeling.*

You may also request waivers of lien, which release you from liabilities for subcontractors and manufacturers. At the end of the job, ask for a final lien waiver for each person who worked on the project so that you are protected from any third-party debts and obligations. It's also a good idea to ask your contractor for a signed affidavit stating that all contractors have been compensated. You don't want to be legally forced to pay for a job twice because your general contractor didn't make good on his debts. With a lien waiver, you can refer an unpaid subcontractor to the general contractor for payment.

Furthermore, don't allow anything to happen on your property that is not in writing. If you want a change, get a written "change order." Remember, any change—whether initiated by you or a supplier or vendor—will cost more money. That's the nature of the game. Every change order should clearly describe what is to be done and how much it will cost. It should also include an estimate of how long it will take to complete the new work and its impact on the production schedule and project time line.

FOUR: *Review licenses, insurance, and permits.* Ask to see the remodeler's license, if your local or state government requires one. However, just seeing it is not enough. It normally won't show expiration or suspension notices. Call the licensing agent to verify the status of the license.

All contractors should have current liability insurance and worker's compensation. The insurance protects employees of the remodeling firm while they are working on your property, so it pays to check it out before you allow possibly uninsured workers to place themselves in hazardous situations in and around your home. If you are still worried about your liability should an injury occur, talk to your insurance carrier and attorney. You may want to adjust your homeowner's coverage during the project.

signing a contract without any liability *if* the contract was obtained some place other than the designer's or contractor's office—your home, for example. This grace period protects you against hasty decisions and hard sells. Federal law mandates making consumers aware of the right to cancel the contract without penalty. Ask your contractor about it.

Also, never allow the work on your home to be done without a legal permit. Permits may cost money and require inspections, but they can save you thousands in the future. In some states, if you have any work done without one and a problem occurs, you are held responsible. Years may go by, but when a tragedy such as a fire happens, you can bet that your insurance agency and the fire marshal will investigate all the causes. If faulty electrical work done during your kitchen remodeling is to blame, the insurance company can refuse to pay the claim if there is no permit on record. This could be disastrous if the entire house burns down. Remember: Nowhere in the home is the possibility of fire more likely than in the kitchen, the place for which more building codes exist than any other room in the house. By obtaining a permit for your remodeling project, you are guaranteeing that a third party will inspect the work to make sure it complies with all safety regulations.

FIVE: *Have it your way.* It's your house and your money. Don't hesitate to ask as many questions as you like about

Smart Tip about Contracts

You have the right to a specific and binding contract. The more details and pages in it, the better. Get specifics on every part of the project and on every product purchased. It is the details that will save you in the long run. Every contract should include basic items, such as

- The contractor's name and proper company name, as listed on the business license
- The company's address, telephone number, and fax number
- The company's business license number if applicable (Some states don't require licensing. If this is the case, find out the company's business license and verify it.)
- Details of what the contractor will and will not do during the project, such as daily cleanup around the site, final cleanup, security measures to be taken during the demolition phase, and so on
- A detailed list of all materials and products to be used, including the size, color, model, and brand name of every specific product (If you have written specifications, you'll need two signatures to change them—yours and the contractor's.)
- The approximate start date and substantial completion dates during the project (You might ask for estimated completion dates for various stages; for example, one-third, halfway, and two-thirds through the process.)
- Your signature required on all plans before work begins (This prevents last-minute changes being made without your knowledge. It also prevents any misunderstandings. This way, you get a chance to look at the plans one last time before walls come down and cabinets and sinks are placed on the wrong side of the room. One drawback to this provision is that it could cause delays if you are out of town during the renovation or are slow to respond. You may want to provide an address where you can be reached by overnight carrier or designate someone to sign in your absence.)
- Notification of your Right of Recision
- Procedures for handling changes in the scope of the work during the course of the project (The procedures should state how change orders will be handled by the contractor. Change orders should require both your signature and the contractor's.)
- A listing and full description of warranties that cover materials and workmanship for the entire project (Warranties are normally in force for one year. They should be identified as either "full" or "limited." A full warranty covers full repair of faulty products or replacement, or your money is returned. A limited warranty indicates that replacements and refunds of damaged products are limited in some regard. Restrictions in limited warranties should be spelled out.)
- A binding arbitration clause in case of a disagreement (Arbitration enables both parties to resolve disputes quickly and effectively without litigation.)
- A provision for contractor's statements and waivers of liens to be provided to you prior to final payment

Include anything else that needs to be spelled out clearly. Remember: If it isn't in writing, it does not exist legally.

Most important, before signing any contract, be sure you understand all the components. You have the right to ask questions and to demand explanations. Never, ever, sign an incomplete contract.

Above: *Exquisite materials and products contribute greatly to the beauty of this unique kitchen design. That's why it is so important that someone be responsible for making sure everything that is ordered for your new kitchen is delivered correctly and in good condition. Let your contractor shoulder that part of the job, as well.*

any detail concerning the project. The more information you have, the happier you will be with the result. This is particularly true when selecting products or figuring out warranty coverage. Find out what is allowed under any warranties and what is forbidden. Many manufacturers won't honor a warranty on an amateur "fix-it" job. To avoid disasters, call your contractor or the manufacturer for guidance.

Make your contractor sign for all deliveries during a job unless you personally ordered the materials or are prepared to be liable for them. Signing for materials is the contractor's responsibility. Imagine what would happen if you

Above: *A granite countertop is a luxury that requires skilled installation. Before signing the contract, make sure it includes a full description of the warranties that cover workmanship, as well as materials.*

Opposite: *Even a small change in the work, such as redesigning part of the cabinetry to incorporate a last-minute addition like a wine rack, requires a written change order.*

signed for an incomplete shipment or the wrong-size floor tiles. That's right, you're responsible for the mistake. Don't take chances. Let your contractor shoulder the burden of tracking down incomplete or damaged orders.

Also, the people you hire to work on your house are in your home. You have every right to tell them not to smoke, play music, curse, or eat inside. You even have the right to tell them where to park and how to store their tools and materials around the place. Of course, you don't want to be unreasonable, but don't be completely put out either. Establish a set of rules before the work begins, and ask the general contractor to enforce them. If he or she doesn't, do it yourself. Include your rules as part of the contract so you have a vantage point from which to operate.

SIX: *Talk the talk.* There is nothing more frustrating than trying to communicate with someone who doesn't speak your language. That is how it can feel, sometimes, when you're trying to talk to someone outside your profession. We all have our own jargon and feel at a disadvantage if we can't use the language of the trade. If you are going to remodel, check out the glossary in the back of this book for commonly used terms in kitchen remodeling.

In addition, decide how you are going to convey problems to your contractor. Again, if you know how you will respond if something goes wrong, you won't panic. If you don't handle stress well, someone else in the household should take over the day-to-day communication with the contractor; maybe your talents could be better spent in the early planning stages and the final decoration.

SEVEN: *Prepare yourself emotionally.* Remodeling is stressful, even if you do the work yourself (perhaps *especially* if you do the work yourself). It's hard to deal with the sawdust and noise and constant inconvenience of not having a finished kitchen. At times it will seem like the project is something that is being done *to* you, rather than *for* you. But there are ways to ready yourself and your family for the temporary upheaval that could last weeks or even a few months.

Begin by talking to everyone in the family about what is involved. If there will be strangers in the home, let everyone meet them before the project begins. Your house is your most personal asset and your most private retreat. It is essential that you and your family know how to protect it and yourselves before there are unfamiliar faces walking in and around the place for extended periods of time. Also, plan ahead for those times when the kitchen is completely off limits. Include a stipend in your budget for restaurant meals and take-out food.

Contractors often talk of what they call the "remodeling curve"—the wave of ups and downs everyone involved in remodeling goes through. Some days are good (such as

Smart Tip about Permits

If your contractor asks you to apply for the permit yourself, refuse. Most jurisdictions consider the person who obtained the permit to be the general contractor and *the one responsible for the outcome of the job.* The county or building officials in your jurisdiction will come to you if the work is not up to code during the inspection. If these officials have a problem, it is far better to let them talk to a professional.

If you are doing the work yourself, be sure to find out the laws in your particular area. Some types of work require that a licensed professional meet code; many jurisdictions won't accept amateur work on electrical systems, for example, because the result of an error can be tragic.

Whether you use a professional or not, get a copy of the permit and keep it in your files for future reference.

Above: *An interior designer helped the homeowner choose the cabinet style, wallpaper, and furnishings.*

Opposite: *A certified kitchen designer planned the space and made the recommendations regarding products and materials.*

when the framing is done) and some days are bad (when it looks as if nothing has happened in days). This is normal. What helps is to talk with your family about it, expect it, and prepare for it. Decide ahead of time to get away for a few days when you feel as if nothing is going the way everybody would like, even if it's just for the weekend. You can

stave off the frustration by anticipating it, and you'll feel more in control if you have a plan of action.

EIGHT: *Evaluate your do-it-yourself skills.* This analysis is a great idea if you are contemplating doing the renovation yourself. We have all seen the various do-it-yourself (DIY) cable shows that make everything look so easy. But don't forget that those shows are run by professionals who have the tools, experience, and skills to do it successfully the first time. Can *you* remodel the kitchen on your own? That depends. The National Association of the Remodeling Industry (NARI) offers a quiz to determine whether you should try the task yourself or leave it to a professional.

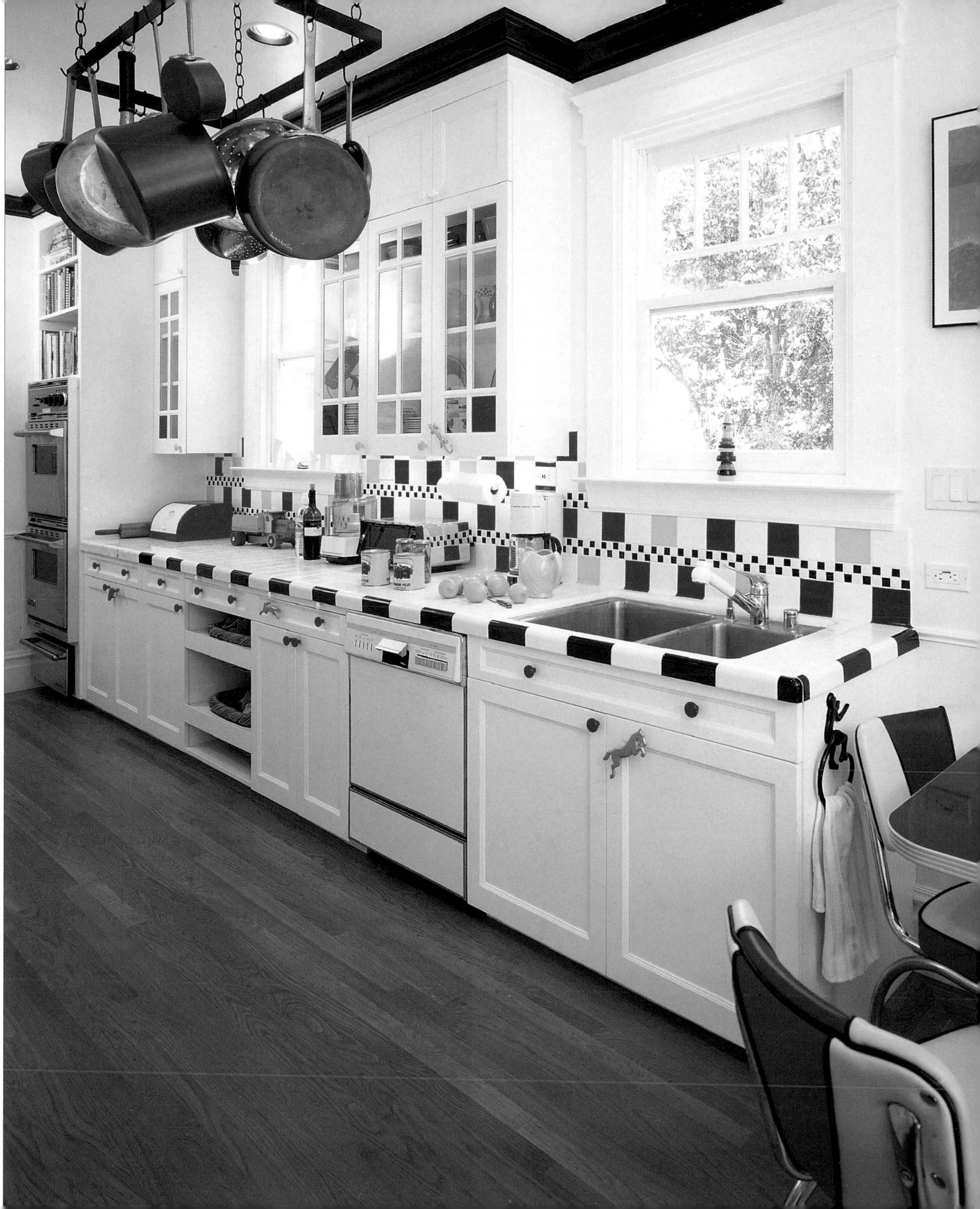

Opposite: *There are few people who can tackle every aspect of a kitchen remodeling. This one involved the skills of numerous subcontractors including cabinet, tile, and flooring specialists.*

Right: *The homeowners made lots of creative contributions, such as finding and refinishing a 1950s dinette set, which inspired the fun tile design.*

Take the test: Circle the answers, and judge for yourself.

Yes No   Do you enjoy physical work?

Yes No   Are you persistent and patient? Do you have reliable work habits? Once the project is started, will it get finished?

Yes No   Do you have all the tools needed and, more importantly, the skills required to do the job?

Yes No   What level of quality do you need for this project? Are your skills at that level?

Yes No   Do you have time to complete the project? (Always double or triple the time estimated for a DIY project, unless you are highly skilled and familiar with that type of project.)

Yes No   Will it matter if the project remains unfinished for a period of time?

Yes No   Are you prepared to handle the kind of stress this project will create in your family relationships?

Yes No   Have you done all of the steps involved in the project before?

Yes No   Have you obtained the installation instructions from the manufacturers of the various products and fixtures to determine whether this is a project you still want to undertake? (You can obtain them from most manufacturers before purchase to determine the steps involved in installation and the skill level required.)

Yes No   Is this a job you can accomplish completely by yourself, or will you need assistance? If you'll need help, what skill level is involved for your assistant? If you need a professional subcontractor, do you have access to a skilled labor pool?

Yes No   Are you familiar with local building codes and permit requirements? (Check into these matters before beginning work on the project.)

Yes No   What will you do if something goes wrong and you can't handle it? (Most contractors are wary about taking on a botched DIY job, and many just won't. The liability is too high.)

Yes No   Is it safe for you to do this project? (If you are unfamiliar with roofing [for a kitchen addition] or do not have fall-protection restraints, you may not want to venture a roofing job. Similarly, if you know nothing about electricity, leave it to the professionals. Some jobs can have serious consequences if not performed correctly. Your health and safety should be the primary concerns.)

Yes No   Can you obtain the materials you need? Who will be your supplier?

Yes No   Are you attempting to do it yourself for financial reasons? If so, have you looked at all your costs, including the cost of materials, your time, and the tools you need to purchase? If you are new to the DIY game, you may also want to consider the cost to correct any mistakes you may make. Will it still be a cost-saving venture given all of these factors?

Yes No   If you are trying DIY for your personal satisfaction, can you really guarantee a job that will be well done? If it doesn't come out right, how will you feel? Will you need the money to redo any unsatisfactory work? Will you have it? Will you be able to live with mistakes?

NARI says that if you marked a majority of the answers "yes," you may want to attempt doing the job yourself. But before you strap on a carpenter's belt, revisit those questions marked "no." Carefully consider the potential problems you will face in those areas if you proceed. Hiring a professional may still be your best option. Or you may want to compromise: Hire a professional for the technical and difficult aspects of the job, and do the cosmetic work yourself. Only you can decide the best course of action for your skill level and project.

For additional advice on whether to try it yourself or work with a professional, you can telephone the NARI Homeowner Remodeling Hotline at 1-800-440-NARI (6274) for a free copy of *The Master Plan for Professional Home Remodeling* magazine, which has additional tests and checklists.

Below: *Although the homeowners weren't qualified to install appliances like this gas cooktop, they shopped for the kinds of appliances that suited their lifestyle and cooking habits.*

Opposite: *The designer found whimsical door and drawer hardware to pull the look together.*

CREATING FUNCTIONAL SPACE

Today's kitchen is often the gathering place for family and friends, the spot where the kids do their homework and you pay the bills, plan the family vacation, design a craft project, or have a heart-to-heart talk with a friend over a cup of coffee. All of that is in addition to the kitchen's traditional function as a place to prepare food. This one room has become so important, in fact, that prospective buyers consider it a primary factor in selecting a home. If you're thinking about remodeling the kitchen for resale purposes, you'll be happy to know you may get as much back as you invest—maybe more, depending on where you live. If you're like most people, however, your motivations are much more personal.

Wouldn't it be delightful to prepare a meal in a kitchen equipped with the latest appliances and configured to let you move effortlessly from refrigerator to sink to cooktop without tripping over the kids, the cat, or your own feet? Imagine opening a cabinet without having to strain or empty the entire contents to find one small can. Picture a countertop that isn't a catchall for the mail, dry cleaning receipts, phone books, dog treats, antacids, and all the rest of cabinet and drawer spillover. Think about enjoying breakfast in a cheery nook filled with morning sunshine or eating quiet dinners in a space that isn't dark, dingy, and in full view of the cooking mess.

Left: *This example demonstrates that a kitchen can be highly organized and functional while retaining an inviting, personal appearance. Warm wood tones and lots of natural light are two of its key ingredients.*

Besides the basics of cooking and cleanup, today's kitchen designs often include room for special pursuits or hobbies. Gourmets grappling with the complexities of gastronomic fare may find professional-style equipment and dedicated work areas handy. The "office" may find a home in the kitchen, too, with space allocated for a desk, computer and printer, and fax machine.

The place to start, then, is with how you want the kitchen to work—for you and every other member of your household. Function is the cornerstone of good kitchen design. A highly functional kitchen will not make you a master chef or change your attitudes about cooking, but it will improve the quality of the time you spend in the kitchen, which some experts report can be as much as 70 percent of your waking hours. With this in mind, remember: Even the smallest remodeling job requires careful planning and

forethought. You can greatly increase the efficiency and performance of your kitchen by paying attention to the tiniest details and the smallest of spaces.

GETTING FOCUSED

Design professionals interview their clients at length at the beginning of a project. If you will be your own designer, do the same. Likewise, you may even want to videotape your family (and yourself) in the kitchen during typical meal preparation or any other kitchen-based activities. If your parties often spill into the kitchen, for instance, videotape the next gathering, and pay attention to how difficult or easy it is to interact with guests while you're cooking or serving. Is there enough room for opening the refrigerator door when someone passes behind you?

Left: *In a kitchen with a vaulted ceiling, the designer made the most of vertical space by specifying small windows for the area on the wall above the cabinets.*

Right: *In another kitchen, the designer situated the cooking area on an outside wall. This arrangement permits easy venting for the range hood, without requiring lengthy ductwork.*

Is there space on the countertop to set up a small, informal buffet or bar so guests can help themselves while you're busy?

Note the different situations that typically interrupt or assist your work flow and traffic patterns. Is the aisle you use to reach the oven the same as the one used to walk from the back door into the house? Observe how many times you have to walk across the room for something.

If you consult with a professional, don't be put off by questions. Any good designer has to get to know the habits,

likes, and dislikes of the people who will live with the finished project. He or she wants to understand your basic requirements in addition to your wildest dreams to meet most, if not all, of your expectations.

A designer will also sketch the existing space to get an idea of what works and what doesn't. This rough drawing may include any adjacent areas that might be considered for expansion, such as a pantry or part of a hallway. Once again, if you act as your own designer, do the same. Talk to everyone in the household. Ask what they think needs improvement, as well as any aspects of the space as it exists that they'd prefer to retain. Find out whether anyone has suggestions for solving any functional problems.

For the best results, approach the project in the same calm analytical manner as a professional, one who understands design and can be objective about what has to happen.

ONE: *Create a design notebook.* It's important to keep all your ideas and records in one place. Buy a loose-leaf binder, and use it to organize everything from magazine clippings to photos of the old kitchen (extremely important if you choose to resell the house); wish lists; notes and interviews with design professionals and family members; contracts; sample plans; shopping lists; color charts; tile, fabric, and wallpaper samples; and anything else related to the project. The file should be comprehensive yet not too clumsy to cart around to kitchen showrooms or stores.

TWO: *Analyze the existing kitchen.* Decide what you *really* want to gain by remodeling. You might begin by asking the most obvious question, "What's wrong with the existing kitchen?" Maybe you and your partner enjoy cooking together, but the floor plan was designed to work for only one cook. Perhaps storage is inadequate or the appliances are old. Or maybe it just looks dated.

To be specific about your analysis, get out your notebook and record answers to questions such as, Is the size of the family likely to grow or shrink in the near future? If the kids are or will be away at college soon, you really might not need that large-capacity refrigerator. Likewise, if this is your first house and you expect to move up as your family size increases, it might be wise to simply refinish high-ticket

items like cabinets and hang onto older appliances that are still in working order, spending only a modest amount of money, time, and energy on cosmetic changes.

Note how each family member uses the kitchen. How many really cook? What kind of meals? Full-course dinners? Microwaveable snacks? Ask everyone, including yourself, to list five items in the current kitchen they couldn't live without and another five items they would gladly give up.

How convenient is it to work in the kitchen? Are people always bumping into each other? When cabinet or appliance doors are open, is the traffic pattern interrupted? Are the sink and countertop at a comfortable height? Are faucet and appliance controls easy to reach and handle? You can change any of these situations to your liking.

Opposite: *This peninsula serves more than one function. First, it effectively separates the work and dining areas of the kitchen. Second, it provides additional counter and storage space without closing up the room.*

Right: *In a small kitchen that accommodates a family that does a lot of entertaining, the island is positioned perpendicular to the location of the aisle in the cleanup area to ease the serving and buffet traffic.*

How many people in the family use the kitchen at the same time? Separate task areas become even more important when two or more people work in the kitchen simultaneously. Who is the main cook? He or she should make the decision about the preferred cooking fuel. Will it be gas, electric, halogen, microwave, or a combination? Keep in mind that the answer will dictate the choice of appliances.

Other questions in your analysis might include: Does the family eat most meals together or separately? Do you need an eat-in kitchen with a built-in booth or a separate dining table, or will a snack island do?

If anyone in the family has physical limitations, implement changes that make the kitchen functional for everyone. (See Chapter Three, "Safety & Universal Design," page 51.)

Is the kitchen too small? Too dark? Can you add on? If not, look at adjacent areas. Is there a pantry, hallway, or part of another room you can incorporate into the kitchen? Would an additional window or skylight make the space feel more open? If you would like to make the kitchen accessible to outdoor living areas, are French doors an option? What other forms of entry are possible?

One common complaint about existing kitchens is the lack of storage. If space limitations have forced you to keep kitchen- or cooking-related items in other rooms of the house, it's time to analyze how to increase the storage capacity in the kitchen. If you go shopping once a month to stock up or shop in bulk, a roomy pantry—perhaps in addition to a large-capacity refrigerator and freezer—may help. Even if you can't increase the total linear feet of cabinetry in the kitchen, you can maximize what you have. On the other hand, if you eat out several nights a week, entertain rarely, or buy produce and meat or fish daily, you might find other uses that are of more importance to you for what would otherwise be storage space.

What else would you like to include in the kitchen if you had the room—laundry facilities, an ironing board, cleaning or craft supplies, pet food? If you have young children who need supervision while you prepare dinner, how about a place to house games, coloring books, crayons, and the like? Would you like to reserve a cabinet—out of your way—for snacks for the older kids and their friends?

Evaluate the condition of existing materials and appliances. How old are they? Are the appliances energy-efficient? Are the walls, floors, and countertops in good condition? If they are just outdated, you'll still probably want to replace or refinish them to add a fresh face to the new design.

There are other issues to think about, as well. You may prefer a design that's open to the family room or other public areas of the house. Others may want to close off the kitchen—and the mess of meal preparation—to everyone but the cook and cleanup crew. Then there are people who almost live in their kitchen. If you are among them, do your guests hang out there during meal preparation? Do you watch TV while mashing the potatoes? Do you pay the bills, paint crafts, or do other chores at the kitchen table?

Left: *Most families want an eat-in kitchen today. When planning space for table and chairs, pay attention to their distance from any walls to allow easy, comfortable seating.*

Opposite (clockwise from top left): *This homeowner planned space for laundry facilities, a home office, and a lowered counter that acts as a table for quick meals.*

Do you need a comfortable chair next to the phone? Would you enjoy a small sofa or a fireplace in the room?

Planning includes taking a realistic look at the future, too. This means anticipating an aging, expanded, or reduced-size household, or perhaps even moving. Weigh these factors with what needs improvement and any other details you don't want to overlook.

THREE: *Make a wish list.* Besides the basic elements, you may want some special features in your new kitchen—a ceramic glass-top range, modular refrigeration, interchangeable cooktop components, or a warming drawer. Perhaps an elegant granite countertop or a gorgeous custom-tiled range hood has caught your eye.

Create a list of all the accouterments you would like to include, whether or not you think you can afford them. When you have a close-to-perfect plan, that's the time to look for areas to trim if your budget is tight. You might opt

Above: *An angled island creates wider aisles around the cooking zone in this kitchen. Extra-tall cabinets that extend to the ceiling free up floor space and store infrequently used items.*

for a countertop fabricated in an affordable stone lookalike and use the dollars saved for something you can't fake, like an energy-efficient window over the sink, a pair of French doors, or a six-burner cooktop with a grill insert.

You'll find lots of ideas about what's on the market, from basic to luxurious, in Chapter Four, "Products & Materials." Review that chapter along with Chapter Five, "Cabinetry & Storage" and Chapter Six "Major Appliances & More." As you compile your wish list, note everything that fulfills your fantasies, as well as practical items. Be sure to visit showrooms and home centers, too. Talk to salespeople and professionals who can tell you about new product introductions, which seem to appear almost daily.

FOUR: *Sketch the old floor plan.* Just like a professional designer, draw an existing floor plan. Do a rough sketch first, and then transfer your drawing to graph paper with grids marked at 1/4-inch intervals. Draw the sketch freehand or with a straightedge, but do it to a scale of 1/2 inch equal to one foot. This base plan, or "base map," as it is called, should record the layout of the space as it exists. Include measurements for everything, from the width of every door to how far the refrigerator protrudes into the room.

Start by taking measurements, beginning with the length and width of the room. Then from one corner, measure the location of windows, doors, and walls. Record the swing of each door. Write each dimension in feet and inches to the nearest 1/4 inch.

Next draw the cabinetry and appliances, and indicate their height. Measure the position and centerline of the sink (showing how far the center of this fixture is from the wall), but don't forget to list its overall length and width. Also, measure the height of the walls.

Include symbols for light fixtures, outlets, and heat registers. Note load-bearing walls, which cannot be moved without compromising structural integrity. If you are thinking about tearing out *any* wall and you don't know whether it is load-bearing, consult an architect.

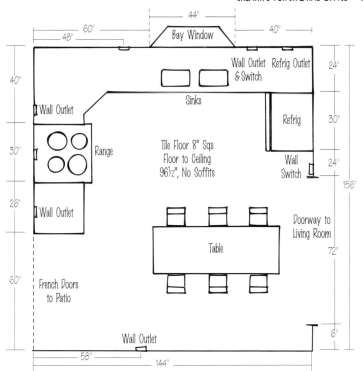

Above: *Make a rough freehand drawing of your existing kitchen, and record accurate measurements as you take them.*

Below: *Transfer information to a scaled drawing on graph paper.*

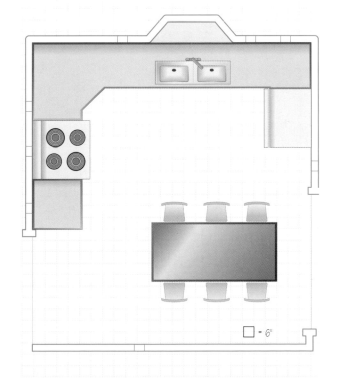

It's a good idea to list your gripes about the old kitchen on the sketch, too. That way you can see at a glance what problems exist and which ones you want to change.

Remember: This floor plan is only a guide. It doesn't have to be professionally drawn, only accurate in its rendition of the current kitchen space.

CONFIGURING SPACE

Whether you are reconfiguring existing space or adding on, the floor plan plays a large role in how well the room will function. And while a kitchen addition to an outside wall of the house offers the best possibilities for unencumbered floor space, it is the costliest option. One way to save money is to restrict your addition to a "bump-out" of 3 feet or less. This doesn't necessarily require a new foundation, and it limits the need for a new roof. Consult an architect or builder, first, to make sure the existing structure is sound and can carry the additional structural load. Remember to inquire about local zoning ordinances that may affect your design before going ahead with plans or construction.

However you choose to proceed, a kitchen of any size requires a thoughtful arrangement of all its elements to make it both highly functional and efficient.

THE WORK TRIANGLE
Almost everybody has heard of the kitchen's classic *work triangle*. Essentially, it is an area that puts the three major work centers—the range, refrigerator, and sink—at the three points of a triangle. The spatial relationship among these sites and how they relate to other areas in the kitchen are what makes the room an efficient work space. In the classic work triangle, the distance between any pair of the three centers is no longer than nine feet and no less than four feet.

To conserve walking distance from point to point without sacrificing adequate counter space, the sum of all three lines of the triangle should be no greater than 26 feet and no less than 12 feet. For a large kitchen, plan two or more

work triangles. Although pairs may extend inside one another, sharing one side or "leg" of the triangle for maximum performance, do not overlap the sink and range areas. An alternative is to design two or more small triangles (work zones) set within one large triangle.

The National Kitchen & Bath Association recommends there be at least one work triangle in a kitchen. In fact, today's busy families—and multipurpose kitchens—often call for two or more separate work triangles. With traditional roles at home changing, so are attitudes about cooking. Two-cook families are more common than ever, and food preparation and cooking have themselves become reasons for social events where even the guests actively participate and everybody helps with the cleanup.

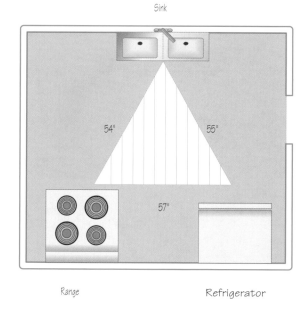

Above: *This design of a work triangle demonstrates good distance limits between the three primary work centers— the range, or cooktop, the refrigerator, and the sink. A larger triangle would require too much walking; a smaller one would create a cramped layout.*

Left: *To enlarge the kitchen and gain space for a dining table and chairs, the owners built an addition onto the back of the house. The wood floor and new, vintage-style cabinetry and hardware is in keeping with the architectural style of the rest of their older home.*

ing an appliance—particularly a small one like the microwave—to a less-busy area. For ideas, take a look at the floor plan examples of typical kitchen traffic problems and their solutions, which appear on the next two pages.

There is some debate, today, among professional kitchen designers concerning the traditional work triangle. Although most agree that it is still an important element, many see the triangular space evolving as cooking habits and lifestyles change. These designers feel that the more actual living done in the kitchen, the more expanded the basic triangle will have to become. And as kitchens grow larger—which appears to be the trend—they will embrace an increasing number of activities. This will result in the need for several autonomous triangles within the room. Whichever school of thought you follow, the bottom line still is and always will be: Design for your sake, not for the sake of design.

ADDING ON

If reorganizing existing space isn't enough, you may have to build an addition. Adding on will raise your budget significantly; it requires excavating and laying a new foundation and installing new plumbing, electrical, and mechanical systems. You may have to supplement or replace your heating system to handle the new load. And you will definitely have to extend the roof. This is a major undertaking.

If reconfiguring your existing space won't solve the problem and the thought of adding on is too daunting or more than you can afford, consider some other options:

Steal Space. Look at areas adjacent to the kitchen, such as hallways, pantries, under the stairs, or even an adjoining room. You may be able to open up the layout or create enough floor space to accommodate an island or peninsula by removing a nonload-bearing wall.

Because a goal of the work triangle is to keep normal kitchen traffic from interrupting the work flow, during your planning stage pay especially close attention to how everyone in the household comes and goes in the existing layout. You might even try this admittedly unusual but enlightening; homespun experiment: Dust the floor with a thin coating of cornmeal; then go about your normal food preparation and cleanup routine. You'll be able to track your movements from cabinets to appliances to sink and the rest of the family's moves around you—or whoever does the cooking. Once you see where the kitchen becomes most crowded, you'll be able to make the necessary changes. (And don't forget to thoroughly sweep up the cornmeal afterward!) Sometimes that's as simple as relocat-

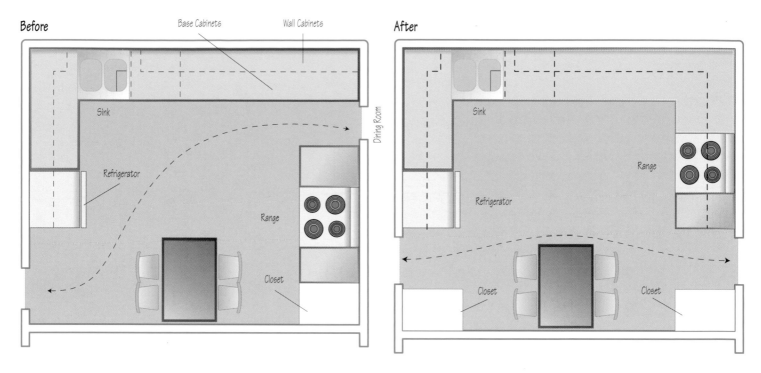

Above: *Doors at opposite corners created diagonal traffic that cut off the range from the sink and refrigerator areas (left). Moving both doors pulls traffic out of the work zone (right). The U-shaped layout puts the refrigerator, sink, and range in a good working arrangement.*

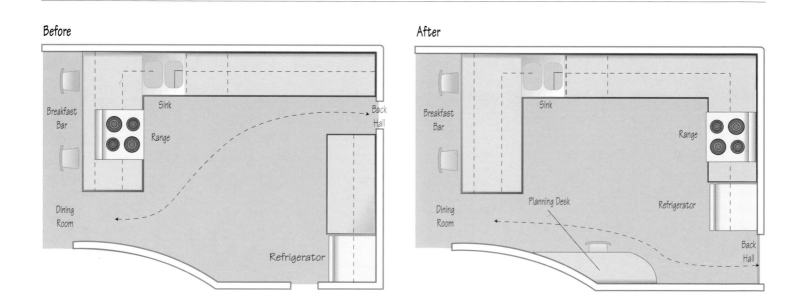

Above: *Open kitchens can have traffic problems, too. Here, the refrigerator is isolated, away from sink and range, and the work area sprawls over a kitchen with too many doors (left). Moving one door and closing another gets traffic out of the work zone (right). Relocating the range makes the breakfast bar much more usable.*

Before

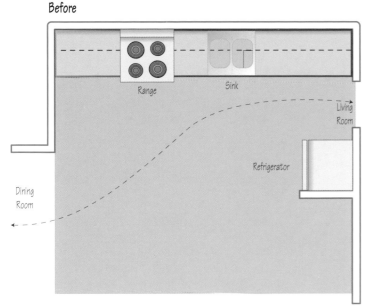

Above: *Old-fashioned kitchens often failed to provide a place to set down food near the refrigerator. Again, traffic interrupts the work zone.*

Below: *Shifting the doorway redirects traffic and allows for more counter and storage space.*

After

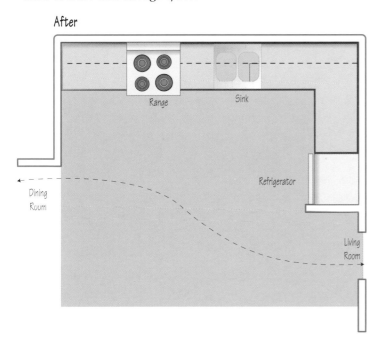

Recess Appliances and Cabinets. You can set custom cabinets as much as 6 inches into the wall between wall studs. Why not do the same for appliances? This doesn't sound like much of a space gain, but 6 inches on each side

of a room may yield enough additional square footage for an efficient work triangle.

Convert. Don't limit your search to interior living space. Take over the garage or porch. Although you'll have to weatherize them, that project is considerably less expensive than building an addition to the house.

Revisit your original base plan and, using a different color, pencil in possible convertible or attachable space.

Relocate. Have you thought about moving the kitchen to another location in the house? Is there a dining room or bedroom on the ground floor you aren't using? This type of remodeling, while perhaps more extensive and more expensive than stealing space from an adjacent room, could be far less costly than building an addition.

ARRANGING A LAYOUT

All you may be thinking of doing is updating appliances, replacing cabinetry, and installing new flooring, counter-tops, and wallpaper. But you may want to think about modifying the layout, at least on paper. During these pre-liminary phases, you have nothing to lose by playing with the idea. You may be surprised to see how much a few minor changes in your floor plan can improve your original layout. As long as you're not moving or adding gas or electrical supply lines, your changes may not be terribly complicated. Try sketching different arrangements to see how they would work.

SMART STEPS

ONE: Make a new base drawing. Like the base drawing you made for the old kitchen, use a $1/2$-inch scale. If you are using a $1/4$-inch grid, each square would then represent a 6-inch square of real floor space. Begin by drawing the outer walls, and then add the windows and doors.

TWO: Make templates of the appliances and cabinets. Paper templates of appliances and cabinets are an easy way

to experiment with different layouts, or you can purchase manufactured design kits or easy-to-use software packages. Otherwise, refer to the Appendix at the back of this book, where you will find templates of typical size cabinets, appliances, and sinks, which you can trace. Cut them out so you can move them around your plan. If you have collected spec sheets (printed product information from manufacturers) for the items you may be purchasing, use the supplied dimensions to create your own templates to scale.

THREE: Place the appliances, fixtures, and cabinetry.

You will use some appliances more often than others: first the sink, next the range, then the refrigerator. Create your work triangles initially, and then specify storage cabinets and counters around them. Indicate all windows and doors; also measure and note the door swing.

Once you have your work triangle(s) arranged, locate auxiliary features, such as the dishwasher, microwave, trash compactor, indoor grill, and oven. If there is any leeway in the plan, place the oven so it doesn't open near a door. (For other safety concerns, check out Chapter Three "Safety & Universal Design.") Don't forget to pencil in all the cabinetry—both upper *and* lower—as well as an island or peninsula or special built-in units such as a desk or pantry. Be sure to include the dining table in an eat-in kitchen and any other freestanding furnishings you expect to use, such as a hutch, sofa, or TV.

Pay particular attention to point-of-use storage. Specify a place to keep spices, pots, and pans near the cooktop; dry goods like flour and sugar at the bake center; and paper and plasticware near the microwave.

A different but valid approach is to place big items first. Start with any large commercial appliances, if you have them, and then work down in size to the small items, which might include the trash compactor or recycling bins.

Opposite: *In this generous layout there was plenty of room for two sinks. One is in the food preparation area, just a few steps away from the cooktop; it is reserved for rinsing produce and filling pots. The second sink is located in the island, which serves as a combination cleanup center and breakfast bar.*

Below: *Because it is typically narrow, a galley (or corridor-style) kitchen works best for one cook at a time. You should allow for a 48-inch-wide aisle, but you can cut it down to 36 inches if space is really at a premium.*

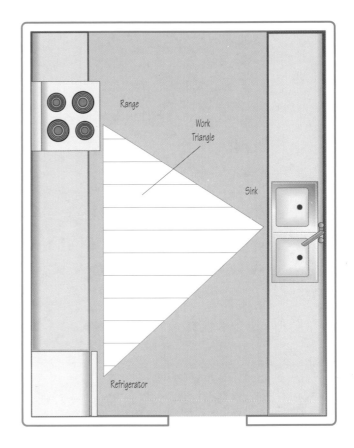

A lot of what you will do is just common sense, such as keeping the dishwasher and refrigerator near the sink for easy cooking and cleanup. If you have space for two or more work triangles with separate sinks, reserve one for the food preparation area and the other for the cleanup zone.

Although function must be uppermost in your mind when designing a kitchen layout, don't forget about aesthetics. Remember the sight lines from outside the room when situating a work zone or a high-traffic area, as well as large appliances such as the sink, stove, and refrigerator. And try to keep the cleanup as far from view from the living area as possible. As you draw your layout, apply the principles of balance and symmetry whenever possible. Center the sink under a window or on a wall, for example.

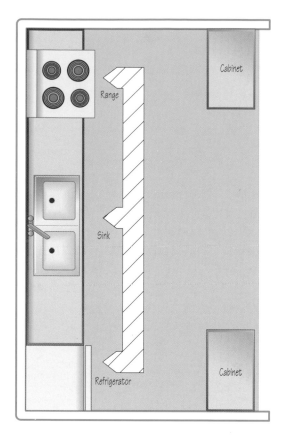

Above: *A kitchen that is configured along one wall requires the least amount of space. To maximize accessibility and allow for two people to use the kitchen at once, place the sink between the cooktop or range and refrigerator.*

Most of all, remember front and side clearances when locating appliances and permanent fixtures. Codes usually require a minimum clearance for each one. Check with your local building department, and ask about regulations for the placement of electrical outlets and appliances, too.

BASIC KITCHEN LAYOUTS

There are five basic kitchen layouts: one-wall, galley (corridor-style), U-shaped, L-shaped, and G-shaped. Each has its challenges and advantages.

One-Wall. This arrangement places all the equipment, sink, and cabinetry along one wall. Because you cannot create a triangle in a one-wall kitchen, maximize accessibility by locating the sink between the refrigerator and the range. Although a one-wall kitchen is more typical in a small apartment, it may be found in a large, open-plan home. If you want to retain this arrangement but would like to close off

the kitchen from other public areas of the house, install sliding doors or screens that can be opened or closed at will.

The Galley. Also known as the *corridor style*, this compact layout locates the appliances, sink, and cabinets on two parallel walls to create a small pass-through kitchen. It's easy to configure an efficient work triangle in this setup, but this layout really caters to one cook. Allow a 48-inch-wide aisle after all fixtures are in place so that cabinet and appliance doors can be opened easily while someone walks through. If space is really tight, you could make the aisle 36 inches wide, but appliance doors may collide with each other if more than one is open at the same time. Another tip: Avoid installing doorways at both ends of the galley or corridor. That way, you can keep people from walking through the work triangle while the cook is busy.

To ease as many traffic problems as possible, place the refrigerator near the end of a galley kitchen—away from the entrance into the room. Another option is to install the primary refrigerator in the food preparation area and a small model for soft drinks or snacks close to the doorway.

Storage is a real challenge in this compact layout. The solution is to install tall cabinets that extend to the ceiling. You'll have to keep a stepladder handy for gaining access to what's on top, so reserve that space for items that you don't use often but want to store in the kitchen.

The L-shape. This plan places the kitchen on two perpendicular walls. The L-shape usually consists of one long and one short "leg," and lends itself to an efficient work triangle without the problem of through traffic. If it's well designed, it's flexible enough for two cooks to work simultaneously without getting in each other's way.

Another advantage to this layout is the opportunity for incorporating an island into the floor plan, if space allows. (Attach a peninsula to one leg of the design, and you've created an F-shaped space.) If you do include an island or peninsula in an L-shaped kitchen, plan the clearances carefully. Walkways should be at least 36 inches wide. If the walkway is also a work aisle, increase the clearance to 42 inches. A 36-inch clearance is fine for counter seating, unless traffic goes behind it. In that case, clearance should be 65 inches.

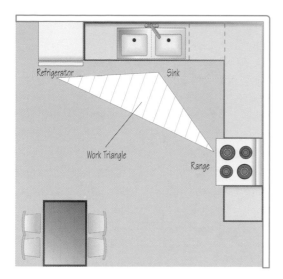

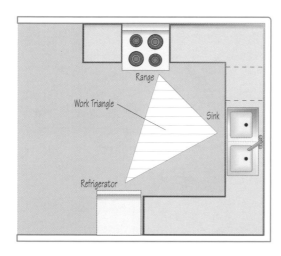

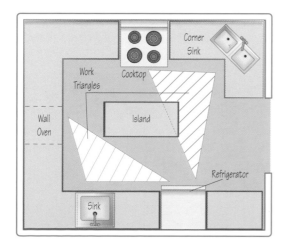

The U-shape. Some experts believe the U-shaped kitchen is the most efficient design, but others say it's a matter of personal preference. Cabinets, counters, and appliances are all arranged along three walls in a U configuration. The greatest benefit, perhaps, is the interrupted space for traffic flow.

A U-shaped layout incorporates a logical sequence of work centers with minimum distances between each. The sink is often located at the base of the U, with the refrigerator and range on the side walls opposite each other. The U shape takes a lot of space—at least 8 feet along the length and width of the kitchen. Corners may be a problem because they often create unusable space. However, you can overcome that by angling cabinets into otherwise "dead" areas. Corner units on the countertop make roomy appliance garages, and bottom cabinets with carousel shelves or Lazy Susans actually make storage more handy than standard units.

Smaller U-shaped kitchens can be dark because of the sheer mass of all that cabinetry. You can overcome this drawback with a generous-size window, skylights, or under-cabinet task lighting, or by keeping surfaces a light color.

The U-shaped kitchen is ideal for two cooks and two work triangles. The work areas may have to overlap somewhat in a smaller layout—meaning two cooks may have to share one leg of the triangle—but it can be done.

The G-shape. This is a hybrid of the U-shape with a shorter, fourth leg added in the form of a peninsula. While the G-shaped layout is suitable for more than person working in the kitchen, it may feel confining—particularly with an island located in the center.

Top: *In a L-shaped kitchen, two intersecting walls are put to work. You can often fit a table or booth into the corner by placing it diagonally opposite the L.*

Center: *A U-shaped design is, perhaps, the most efficient layout and provides the greatest amount of counter space between the sink and appliances.*

Bottom: *Two cooks can easily maneuver around a G-shaped layout, which offers enough room for two work triangles. Both of them are typically anchored at the refrigerator.*

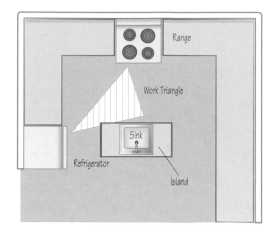

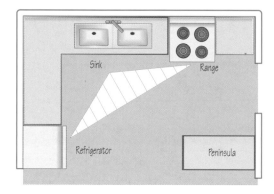

Top: *Depending on the location of utility lines and venting possibilities, either the sink or cooktop can be installed into a kitchen island.*

Bottom: *A peninsula brings counter space and storage conveniently close without interfering with the work triangle. It works well with an L-shaped layout.*

This layout may feature a pair of sinks and a separate cooktop, as well as oven ranges. One work triangle usually incorporates a sink, the cooktop, and the refrigerator, while the other houses the second sink, the oven, and, overlapping the first triangle, the refrigerator.

The G-shaped kitchen often accommodates specialty appliances, such as warming drawers, modular refrigeration, or a built-in grill, to allow as much independence between the two work areas as possible.

ISLANDS AND PENINSULAS

In a roomy layout, you can shorten the distance between the three key work areas by adding an island or peninsula. A peninsula base and ceiling-hung cabinets offer convenient storage for tableware and linens. In an L- or U-shaped kitchen, an island can add visual interest, breaking up the space without confining it. It also provides an extra work surface, a convenient spot for snacks or informal meals, as well as a place for setting up a buffet when entertaining.

An island or peninsula can also serve as an excellent location for a cooktop or second sink, if plumbing and ventilation hookups permit. It could also prove the ideal spot for a wine rack or cooler, a wet bar, warming drawers, modular refrigerator units, or additional general storage. For maximum efficiency, be sure the design provides a clearance of 48 inches from the island or peninsula to the wall cabinets.

EATING AREAS

There are specific minimum clearances you'll need to accommodate a table and chairs, which you mustn't forget to include in a design for an eat-in kitchen. Plan enough floor space for all the furniture and for people to sit down, get up, and walk around the table comfortably, without interfering with the work traffic.

Seating Allowances. If you feel as if you're a contortionist every time you get into or out of your chair at the table, the person who designed the existing kitchen didn't do proper space-planning homework. When you redesign, follow the guidelines here and you won't go wrong.

Even average-size people need a surprising amount of space to make a dining area accessible. Allow 12 to 15 square feet per person. That means a family of four will require at least 48 square feet in an eat-in kitchen. Assume that a 36-inch-diameter round table can seat four adults; a 48-inch-diameter one will accommodate six. Calculate 21 to 24 inches of table space per person for a square or rectangular table.

When planning space for your kitchen table, pay attention to the distance between it and the walls or cabinets. A seated adult occupies a depth of about 20 inches from the edge of the table but will need 12 to 16 *additional* inches of space to push back the chair and rise. This means you have to plan on 32 to 36 inches of clearance between the wall and the edge of the table. You can get away with a minimum of 28 inches if chairs are angled to the wall. However, plan on a 44-inch clearance to allow enough room on any serving side of any table, whatever its shape.

If you don't have enough room for a table, a booth or a table with banquette, or bench, seating may be the answer. A kitchen alcove or bay window offers a natural spot for this type of seating arrangement, or you can back it against an island, peninsula, or wall. Plan 21 inches of table space for each person, with at least 15 inches of knee space underneath. This means that a family of four minimally needs a 42-inch-long table that measures 30 inches across. Because you slide in and out of a booth, the table may overhang the benches by 3 or 4 inches. Total floor space required for a four-person booth, therefore, measures only 5 feet across, compared with a minimum requirement of about 9 feet for a freestanding table with chairs.

Another popular option for in-kitchen dining is to let the island or peninsula serve double duty as an eating bar. Remember, each adult requires at least 21 inches of table space, so that means a 63-inch-long counter (a typical size) will accommodate three stools at most.

Seating depends on counter height. A 28- to 32-inch-high counter requires 18-inch-high chairs with 20 inches of knee space under the bar. If you make the island or peninsula the same height as the rest of the kitchen countertops (36 inches being the standard), you'll be able to accommodate 24-inch-high stools and 14 inches of knee space. Go up to bar height (42 to 45 inches), and you'll need 30-inch-high stools with footrests, also with 14 inches of knee space.

SECONDARY WORK CENTERS

One of the most popular secondary work centers in new kitchens today is the home office. You may place it in another part of the room—away from food preparation tasks—and include a desk, bookcase, and accommodations for a computer, printer, phone, and fax machine. Or you

may want to incorporate it in the main area as part of the built-in cabinetry. That's fine, as long as it's outside the work triangles. If the work surface and storage are designed as part of the kitchen cabinetry, you'll have to drop the counter height to about 30 inches to be comfortable sitting there. If you're purchasing stock cabinets, you should be able to buy 30-inch-high base units for areas that adjoin the desk. These can be used to house supplies and files. Keep the depth of your desk the same as the rest of the countertops so you have one smooth line of cabinetry, but be sure there is a comfortable amount of knee space (approximately 15 inches) underneath.

Serious craft devotees can follow the same advice when planning their hobby work space. Incorporating a roll-top counter appliance garage with an electrical outlet in the design allows you to store a portable sewing machine or other heavy equipment, so you won't have to lift it onto the desk or countertop.

Another specialty area desired by serious cooks, especially bakers, is a bake center. For this space, allocate at least 36 inches near the oven or refrigerator, ideally between the two appliances. Specify 30-inch-high base cabinets, which are a more comfortable height for mixing and kneading. An extra-deep countertop (30 inches or more) will provide plenty of room for rolling out dough.

Gardening enthusiasts may also appreciate a dedicated area away from the bustle of food preparation and cleanup. Equipped with its own sink—and perhaps a window—this space might include a cabinet and drawers to house containers and vases, tools, plant food, and other related items. A convenient arrangement is a counter that measures 36 inches high and a tall chair or stool with 12 inches of knee space.

Locating laundry facilities in the kitchen can be tricky unless you have lots of floor space. Like other appliances with doors, washers and dryers in use can tangle traffic aisles. Another complication: Your washer will most probably have to be placed next to, if not nearby, a sink. If you don't have the room to park these machines in a separate but adjacent nook off the kitchen or in a bathroom, and you don't want to haul dirty laundry to the basement, be sure to place these workhorse appliances thoughtfully. A side-by-side pair of full-size appliances measures 48 to 58 inches in width. Full-size units are also about 6 inches taller than typical counter heights. If you're really pressed for floor space, you might want to think about stackable models.

Once you conclude how you want your new kitchen space to function, you're in a position to tackle the challenge: selecting products, materials, and cabinetry. But first, review the important advice offered in Chapter Three, "Safety & Universal Design."

Above: *Including a table and chairs in your kitchen plan requires providing a 32- to 36-inch clearance between any walls and the edge of the table.*

Right: *A kitchen peninsula can be an excellent solution to creating an informal eating area out of the way of work traffic. The seating depends on the height of the counter, which can be higher or lower than others in the kitchen.*

SAFETY & UNIVERSAL DESIGN

Sharp knives. Intense heat. Electrical appliances in close proximity to water. Hard, unforgiving surfaces. Breakable glassware and china. These are some of the ingredients in a perfect recipe for kitchen accidents. They also represent safety concerns that should be considered during the design stage of your kitchen remodeling. Although this is true under any circumstances, it is particularly important when those who will be using the kitchen are the most vulnerable: children and the elderly.

Universal design addresses the needs of multigenerational households. As Baby Boomers bring home their aging parents while raising families of their own, it is not uncommon to have young children and grandparents living under one roof at the same time. Indeed, as our population ages it benefits everyone to think about ways to make the kitchen functional—and safe—for every member of the family. This chapter addresses all of these concerns and discusses kitchen accessibility for people with special needs.

SAFETY FIRST

More building codes govern the kitchen than any other room in the house. That's because so many accidents occur there. With that in mind, safety should reign as a primary factor in any kitchen remodel. The goal should be to lessen the chance of injury while increasing the performance of the room's layout, materials, fixtures, and appliances.

Left: *Good food and great atmosphere are two important ingredients in this comfortable, inviting kitchen. Safety and ease of use enhance the mix.*

Take the following steps when designing for safety. And remember: You don't have to be very young or very old to suffer an injury in the kitchen. One of the most common Sunday morning hospital emergency room visits is by someone who has sliced open a hand while cutting a bagel.

SMART STEPS

ONE: *Use proper lighting.* Never work in a dim space. Good general lighting, supplemented with proper task lighting clearly focused on a work surface, without glare or shadows, can vastly decrease your chance of injury while preparing a meal. In addition, good lighting should be adaptable to meet the needs of younger, as well as older,

eyes. Review Chapter Seven, "Light by Design," for specific advice regarding how much light you need and where it should be placed for optimal benefits.

TWO: *Use slip-resistant flooring.* Falling with a hot casserole or sharp knife in your hand can have serious consequences. Choose a slip-resistant material for your floor, such as matte-finished wood or laminate, textured vinyl, or a soft-glazed ceramic tile indicated specifically for flooring. If you select tile, it helps to use a throw rug with a non-skid backing—especially around areas that get wet. Remember to inquire about the slip-resistance rating of any flooring material you may be considering for your new kitchen.

Above: *A clear path permits the safe transport of food from the work area to the kitchen table or all the way through to the formal dining room.*

Opposite: *The food preparation and cleanup area of this kitchen is compact so the designer made sure there are no sharp edges around the countertops that could cause injury as people move quickly from the work areas to the table.*

THREE: *Keep a fire extinguisher handy.* A grease fire in the kitchen can spread rapidly. That's why it's so important to have a fire extinguisher within arm's reach of the ovens and cooktop. For maximum protection, there should be at least two extinguishers in any kitchen—one located in the cooking area and one stored in another part of the room. You want them to be handy; however, you don't want fire extinguishers to fall into the hands of children. Install them high enough so that they are out of reach for curious youngsters.

FOUR: *Keep electrical switches, plugs, and lighting fixtures away from water sources and wet hands.* In addition, make sure every electrical receptacle is grounded and protected with ground-fault circuit interrupters. These devices cut electrical current if there is a power surge or if moisture is present. Most building codes require them in any room where there is plumbing to protect homeowners against electrical shock.

FIVE: *Consider lock-out options.* New smart-home technology allows you to lock your range and ovens so no one can use them while you are out of the house. The simple lock-out device can prevent burns, fires, or worse. You can choose between lock-out covers or a programmed lock-out system. Or you can install timers on all appliances you don't want in use when you can't supervise the cooking. Installing guard rails around burners is another good idea.

You might also consider designating one wall cabinet for storing cleansers and other toxic substances—the fire extinguisher, for example. Include a lock on the cabinet, and keep the key in a safe place.

SIX: *Regulate water temperature—and devices.* Install faucets with antiscald devices that prevent water temperature from rising to dangerously high levels, or buy pressure-balanced valves that equalize hot and cold water. Although pressure-balanced faucets were available only in single-lever styles in the past, now some models with separate hot- and cold-water valves offer this safety feature, too. Another option is a faucet that can be preprogrammed to your desired temperature setting. All of these controls should be childproofed with lock-out features.

SEVEN: *Design a safe cooktop.* How many times have you been scalded reaching over a boiling pot or a hot element? Avoid this dangerous situation by selecting staggered burners for your cooktop or one straight row of burners. If you can't find single burners, turn two-burner units sideways, placing them parallel to the front of the countertop. Never choose a unit with controls at the rear of the cooktop; controls should be along the side or in front.

EIGHT: *Use space efficiently and safely.* You can have all the space in the world and still put family members in compromising situations. Avoid swinging doors. When

Above: *Reserving space under the cooktop for pots and pans on open wire shelving makes items easily accessible. A safety rail in front of the burners helps to maintain a guarded distance from open flames.*

Opposite: *Wide aisles and the angled position of the range prevents hazards when oven doors are open.*

placing appliances, think about how the traffic area will be affected when a door is open. Locate ovens and the microwave at a comfortable height that doesn't necessitate reaching in order to retrieve hot food. Install carousel shelves, Lazy Susans, and slide-out trays and bins in base cabinets to make storage more accessible without doing a lot of bending.

Avoid sharp corners, especially at the end of a run of cabinetry or on the island or peninsula. If space is tight and you can't rearrange most elements, install a rounded end cabinet and choose a countertop material that will allow a bull-nose edge treatment—a solid-surface product, for example.

UNIVERSAL DESIGN

As people age, their capabilities change; some become more challenged than others and need more assistance with day-to-day chores. Universal design is an approach that adapts the home to people of all skills. It evolved as a response to our increasingly aging society.

Incorporating universal design into your remodeling is always smart, particularly if you plan to stay in your house as you grow older. Analyze your lifestyle and your family's needs now—*and* what you anticipate them to be in the future. Do you have young children? Do you expect to have an elderly parent living with you? Will you remain in the

Opposite: *These specialty cabinets, designed to meet the needs of the physically challenged, feature base cabinets that accommodate a raised dishwasher, lowered wall oven, and knee room under the sink and cooktop.*

Left: *A tambour-door unit, located in a base cabinet next to the oven, holds small appliances and pans for easy access.*

Below: *The table pullout fully extends for an accessible work or eating surface.*

house after you retire? Planning to include some universal-design features in your new kitchen now will save you money later on, because it's more expensive to make changes to an existing plan.

According to the NKBA, one of the easiest and most practical universal-design elements you can include is the installation of counters at varying heights, which allows you to perform some tasks (slicing vegetables, for example) while seated and others (such as rolling out dough) while standing, not bending. Another idea that makes sense for any kitchen is a pull-out counter near both the cooktop and another at the oven. They provide handy landing places for hot pots, pans, and dishes. Or design a compact work triangle that eliminates the need for extra steps. For most people, an L-shaped layout accomplishes this most efficiently. (See Chapter Two, "Creating Functional Space.") However, individual lifestyles will dictate their own preferences. Other ideas include choosing digital displays, which are easier to read and fairly standard on today's appliances;

placing wall-mounted switches and outlets at the universal reach range of 15 to 48 inches from the floor; reserving a base cabinet for storing dishes, making dinnerware easier to reach; installing wrist-blade-style faucets that don't require grabbing or twisting; and buying a side-by-side style refrigerator, which places most foods at accessible heights.

It might also be worthwhile to investigate some of the smart-home technology available. This includes devices that allow you to call home from any phone to turn on the lights, heat the oven, raise the thermostat, or program dinner to start cooking. Of course, this sophisticated technology is expensive and may be more practical for new construction; some things are too complicated to retrofit into an existing home. New technological advances are brought to the marketplace every week. The key is to look at universally designed features and match them to your home and situation. Don't forget: The goal is to make your life easier—and safer. If adding any of these features will destroy your budget or drastically change your concept of

Smart Tip about Electrical Outlets and Switches

Sometimes the special needs of the disabled may seem to conflict with those of the very young. A case point is accessible switch and outlet placement, which is lower on a wall. As an alternative, the NKBA recommends locating them inside the front of a tilt-down drawer to conceal them from children. Alternatively, an outlet strip can be kept out of a child's reach and at a convenient adult location while lessening the reach to plugs and switches installed in the backsplash.

the room, don't use them, but retain any features that can save your family pain or injury.

You may have heard the terms accessible and adaptable design used interchangeably and with universal design. However, all of these are different. You've just learned about universal design; here's an explanation of the other two.

ACCESSIBLE DESIGN

Accessible design normally means that a home—or in this case a kitchen—is barrier-free. It also indicates that the room complies with design guidelines for disabled people found in government regulations such as the American National Standards Institute's A117.1 (ANSI A117.1-1986). There are a number of guidelines governing accessible design. Their goal is to provide criteria for designing for the wheelchair-bound. Most accessible homes incorporate a number of fixed features that give a disabled person easy access.

If a disabled person in your family will use the new kitchen, plan the space accordingly, making sure there is adequate room for that person to move around. Design appropriate clearances. A standard wheelchair occupies 10 square feet and has a turning diameter of 5 feet. Therefore, doorways must be at least 32 inches wide, and aisles must be a minimum of 42 inches wide, according to the NKBA.

A lowered cooktop with an angled nonfogging mirror installed above the surface lets someone seated see what's cooking. If you don't like the look of an open space below the cooktop, install retractable doors that open to accommodate the wheelchair and close for a finished look. An induction cook-

top is probably the most practical choice for this situation. It features an automatic shutoff, has a cool-to-the-touch cooking surface, and is easy to keep clean. (See Chapter Six, "Major Appliances and More.") Low, shallow base cabinets outfitted with pull-out and slide-out bins and trays, carousel shelves, and Lazy Susans maximize accessibility, as do lower counter heights—31 inches as opposed to the standard 36 inches. Light-colored countertops with a contrasting edge treatment that clarifies where the surface ends are recommended for people with impaired vision.

At least one American cabinet manufacturer has introduced a line of specially designed cabinets and accessories that accommodate everyone in the family, including those with special needs. Features include a lowered base cabinet; an oven cabinet accessible from a seated position; a raised dishwasher enclosure for easy loading and unloading; a sink base that allows seated use but conceals plumbing; a 9-inch-deep toe-kick to permit wheelchair access; a tambour-door base cabinet unit; base microwave cabinets; and knife hinges for barrier-free door opening. Each one of these features reflects an idea that should be designed into any all-accessible kitchen.

You might also want to consider having a second microwave near the kitchen table. The cabinet you choose to house it should have a drop-down door, to provide a shelf for resting hot dishes straight from the oven.

And if you have the space, keep one or two rolling carts in the kitchen that allow someone to easily transport several items around the room—especially foods on large serving platters—at the same time.

ADAPTABLE DESIGN

Adaptable design refers to features that can be easily modified for use by a disabled person. Such design features are normally found in multifamily rental housing so that a landlord is able to rent to anyone. The adaptable-design kitchen incorporates some concealed traditional accessible features— for example, doors under the sink that can be removed to allow accessibility for someone in a wheelchair.

Opposite: *To make this kitchen accessible for a wheelchair-bound homeowner, the designer specified drop-down cabinet doors that double as landing surfaces, a deep toekick, and knee space under the counter. Note the convenient placement of the electrical outlet.*

SHOPPING FOR PRODUCTS & MATERIALS

The products you select to outfit your new kitchen will affect both your design and your budget. If you choose top-of-the-line materials, expect a top-of-the-line bill. Factors that influence the cost of new appliances, cabinetry, countertops, and flooring include updated technology and type of finish. The smarter the device, the more you'll pay for it. Likewise, the fancier the finish, the higher the price tag. But cost doesn't always reflect quality, nor does it equate necessarily with satisfaction. And quality and personal satisfaction are the two most important factors in making all of your decisions about product selection.

How can you make smart choices about items like cooktops and dishwashers, sinks and faucets, countertop materials and flooring? How can you tell whether a product is reliable, whether it will endure and take the daily abuse? Are there basic differences that make one faucet or a particular type of dishwasher better than another? To find out, you can do a little research. Shop around. Visit showrooms, read, and don't be afraid to ask questions. If you don't, you'll have to take your chances. If you're not the gambling type, however, here are steps you can take to select products and materials for your new kitchen with confidence.

Left: *An important part of your remodeling project involves shopping for the best products and materials for your kitchen. The tile, countertop, and faucet all bring style and convenience to this design.*

ONE: *Separate the product from the hype.* A high price tag doesn't always mean high quality. Find out what's different about one refrigerator that costs $800 and another that sells for $1,200. (See Chapter Six: "Major Appliances & More.") That way you can decide whether the higher-priced model is worth it. A knowledgeable salesperson will be able to tell you. If not, contact the manufacturer. Many have 800 numbers and web sites specifically set up to answer consumer questions. Sometimes the high price is because of a feature you can't see. For example, a faucet with replaceable parts costs much more than one with parts that can't be replaced. How much do you want to gamble that the faucet you buy won't break?

TWO: *Weigh your options.* Analyze the pros and cons that come with each product. Once you have that information, reaching a decision will be easier. For example, if you are sprucing up an old kitchen or adding a new one in a house you expect to sell soon, you might install a less-expensive countertop material. But if you are making a major investment in a remodeling project that you plan to live with for a long time, you will be happier in the long run with an item that may cost more but will give you great satisfaction and be reliable for years to come.

THREE: *Seek sound advice.* Ask the manufacturer about the expected lifespan of the product and its efficiency. Don't take advice from a store clerk if he or she is not an experienced remodeling professional. Talk to your contractor. He may be familiar with the product or can pass along critical feedback about it from other clients.

FOUR: *Don't make a choice based solely on style or color.* It doesn't work for cars, and it won't work for building materials or appliances. Sure, style and color are important, but it's just as easy to find a first-rate appliance that looks great in your new kitchen as it is to find one that

Opposite: *You'll notice a great price range for most materials and appliances. Find out why. A granite countertop is luxurious and priced accordingly*

Left: *This solid-surface countertop isn't quite as expensive as natural stone, but it does cost more than standard plastic laminate, which isn't as durable.*

Above: *It isn't difficult to find good looks in every price range today. A graceful gooseneck faucet is attainable for most budgets, but make sure the valving is top quality.*

Opposite: *Affordable standard plastic laminate can be perked up with special edge trim to make it look richer.*

looks fabulous but performs poorly. Keep function and quality as your primary criteria for selecting products.

FIVE: *Prorate costs.* You may be dismayed by the price of some items, but when you divide the cost of the product or material by its anticipated longevity (how many years you expect it to last), you may be amazed at how reasonable the price is. Of course, this won't alleviate an immediate cash-flow problem, but it will ease some of the sticker shock. An expensive product that will last for 20 years may be a better choice than a cheaper one that may have to be replaced in 5 years. Again, weigh that decision against how long you plan to stay in the house. Are the extra benefits worth spending the extra money?

SIX: *Inquire about guarantees and service options.* Some offers are definitely better than others. Look at the warranty that comes from the manufacturer, as well as those offered by the place of purchase. A store may offer immediate replacement of the entire unit. While this may sound great, it isn't if you have to pay for labor or schedule time off from work for the removal and reinstallation of a tile or fixture. If all that is wrong with a faucet is a faulty washer, you may not want to yank out the entire unit. It should be your call. Find a place that offers a warranty based on the problems with the product. Ask about options in warranty coverage, and always get written copies of all warranties from the store or your contractor.

SEVEN: *Do a reality check.* Evaluate your situation, and choose the best products and materials for the way you live. Don't get swept away by bells and whistles that can blow your budget. A professional range with warming drawers and extra burners may appeal to your gourmet fantasy, but if your cooking routine consists of heating up last night's take-out food, invest the extra money elsewhere.

EIGHT: *Leave nothing to chance.* Investigate every option and every detail. Don't find yourself bemoaning what you should have done once it's too late. After you have signed the final check is not the time to realize you could have installed a wall-mounted pot-filler faucet over your cooktop. Discover everything that's out there—before getting started. Don't miss any of the fun stuff, and you won't have any regrets or extra charges for changes made after work has begun.

The kitchen is the most popular room in the house to remodel, and trends indicate that it will continue to be so for years to come. It is also the place most prospective homeowners look first when deciding whether to buy. New products and design innovations are emerging constantly. You owe it to yourself to investigate every option thoroughly. In Chapter Six, "Major Appliances & More," you'll read about the choices in kitchen equipment, from the most basic to high-performance models. Now here's what you need to know about the latest introductions in fixtures, faucets, and surfacing materials.

COUNTERTOP MATERIALS

Selecting countertop material is not as simple as it once was because there are infinitely more choices in color, pattern, and texture thanks to new materials and applications. The trend is to use more than one material, specifying types based on the functions at hand. For example, you might use a solid-surfacing material in one part of the kitchen, a marble insert at the bake center, and stainless steel next to the cooktop. Or you could pair one countertop material with the cabinetry that runs along the wall, and choose another for the island counter.

In addition to enhancing the function of your work surfaces, the countertop materials you choose can underpin your decorating theme. Wood is a natural choice for a country-style kitchen, for example, whereas concrete looks handsome in a contemporary setting. The concrete can be poured into a mold on site or prefabricated. You can add color to it or create a one-of-a-kind inlaid design with stones, shards of glass, china, tile, shells, or just about anything else you can think of.

There are no hard-and-fast rules about any material you choose, but one important factor that should play a role in your selection is maintenance. Some materials demand greater care than others. Marble, for instance, must be sealed periodically because it can absorb liquids that will mar its looks. If you don't have time for the upkeep, can you live with the battle scars of everyday use?

Here's a rundown on your choices for countertop material. After you've read about the attributes of each, you can decide which ones may be right for your application. Also, consider each type as a possibility for a matching or entirely different backsplash.

PLASTIC LAMINATE

There are probably more homes with plastic laminate kitchen counters than any other surface. Made of several layers of melamine, paper, and plastic resin bonded under heat and pressure, then glued to particleboard or plywood, it's inexpensive, relatively easy to install, and available in a vast array of colors and patterns. Plastic laminate resists stains, water, and mild abrasion very well, but it can be chipped or scratched by sharp knives, and it will scorch if you put a hot pot down on it. There is no repair option available except replacement.

More expensive color-through, or solid-core, laminates are similar to conventional laminate. However, because the color is solid all the way through, there are no unsightly black edges at the joints. Plus, you can layer and rout the edges of solid-core laminates to create decorative effects.

In addition to solid colors, there are laminates that offer the look of stone, leather, or wood, as well as patterns and visu-al textures. Small-scaled speckled patterns are popular today, and they easily camouflage minor scratches and spots. For the health-conscious, at least one manufacturer is offering a plastic laminate that features built-in antibacterial protection. The company claims that the treatment will not wash out and that it keeps bacteria, mold, and mildew from growing on your countertop. Colors are limited now, but look for more variety and some patterns in the near future.

Below: *Solid-surfacing material is versatile. The edge of the countertop, here, features an inlaid pattern.*

Opposite: *Ceramic tile always makes a big design statement. The owner of this kitchen created the black-and-white checkered pattern to suggest the look of a Viennese bakery.*

Plastic laminate comes in various grades. Because it is generally affordable, don't skimp by purchasing the cheapest one you can find. To get your money's worth, select the highest quality, which won't chip easily and stays looking good longer. To keep it clean, use a mild detergent and damp sponge. Unless you seriously burn or scratch the surface, this countertop will last 10 to 15 years.

SOLID-SURFACING MATERIAL

This is an extremely durable, easily maintained synthetic material made of polyester or acrylic. It's expensive, costing almost as much per linear foot as luxurious granite or marble, but it wears long and well. The material is completely impervious to water, and you can repair any dents or abrasions that may occur with a light sanding. At first, solid-surfacing material was available only in shades of white or pastel colors, but now its palette has expanded and includes faux-stone finishes. Because the color goes all the way through the thickness of the slab, it can be carved, inlaid, shaped, molded, even sandblasted to create a custom design.

Maintaining this countertop is easy using a mild nonabrasive cleanser and damp sponge. With a minimum amount of care, it will last 20 or more years.

CERAMIC TILE

Ceramic tile is a perennial favorite. Impervious to water, it's perfect for installation at the sink. Tile is also durable, and it doesn't scratch, burn, or stain. Aside from its practical attributes, ceramic tile offers the greatest opportunity for adding color, pattern, and texture to your kitchen. Custom designs bring personality into the room. Hand-painted, imported, and antique versions are pricey, but you can combine inexpensive standard tiles with raised or silk-screened patterns to create unique designs and murals nonetheless. Combine them with any of a variety of trim tiles, including bullnosed tile, ropes, and accent strips to achieve a custom look at an affordable price range, although installation by a qualified tile setter is not cheap. (Don't overlook metal tiles—chrome and copper—which can be paired with ceramic tiles and coordinate well with today's stainless-steel

appliances and countertops, as well as shiny or matte-finished copper range hoods and sinks.) Ceramic tile comes in an assortment of sizes and shapes (squares, triangles, rectangles, and octagons).

When shopping, you should also consider the finish. There are two kinds: unglazed and glazed. Unglazed tiles are not sealed and always come in a matte look. They are not practical for use near water unless you apply a sealant. On the other hand, glazed tiles are coated with a material that makes them impervious to water—or spills and stains from other liquids, too. This glaze on the tile can be matte or highly polished, depending on your taste.

The upkeep of tile is fairly easy. You must regrout periodically, however. White grout shows dirt easily, but a dark-color one can camouflage stains. Still, unless it is sealed, grout will harbor bacteria. So clean the countertop regularly with a nonabrasive antibacterial cleanser. Tile that is well-maintained and regrouted when needed will last a lifetime, but beware: your glassware and china may not. If you drop them on this hard surface, they'll break.

STONE

Marble and granite are probably the most expensive materials you can choose for a countertop. Though it is stone, marble is actually a soft, porous material that can be gouged and stained easily. Even water leaves a mark. Still, it's a beautiful choice, and you will continue to appreciate it—even the little imperfections it may acquire over time—if you keep it properly sealed and treat it gently.

Marble's cool surface makes it an excellent choice for a countertop material in a bake center or as a pull-out slab that can be opened when needed. Just don't chop or slice food on it, and keep it clean. A marble countertop can serve you—and your kitchen—well for a lifetime.

Considered chic today, a granite countertop is a handsome status symbol. Like marble, it has a cool surface that pastry makers favor, but it is less absorbent. This makes it less

Opposite (clockwise): *Molded concrete with a raised-pattern motif along the backsplash, coarse-grained granite, black granite, illustrate the different ways stone materials can be used creatively at the counter area.*

likely to stain than marble. However, dark colors show fingerprints easily. Granite, too, lasts a lifetime and should be sealed for wear.

Two other stone materials, limestone and concrete, are finding their way onto countertops in the hands of creative designers. Unlike the refined looks of granite and marble, these materials have a rustic, textured appeal. As with all natural materials, they are absorbent and must be sealed. Limestone is available as tiles, as is concrete, but the latter can be poured and molded, too. Becoming even more creative, designers are adding color to concrete. Some applications are carved or routed, even inlaid with tile or stone for an abstract look. Be cautious, however: Concrete cracks very easily. And as with ceramic tile, glass or china dropped on any stone surface will shatter.

WOOD

Wood is unrivaled for its natural warmth and beauty. But it expands and contracts, depending on environmental conditions, and may warp if exposed to water. To protect a wood countertop, apply a film finish of varnish or lacquer or oil it periodically. A film finish seals the wood, but it can crack and get water under it, which will cause peeling. You'll have to sand and reapply the coating every year. If you plan to chop or cut on it, treat the wood with mineral oil, instead. Apply it every few months. When burns or stains occur, they can be sanded away.

Teak is an excellent selection for a wood countertop application. It's handsome and wears well. Another option is butcher block, which is actually a laminated wood product. Durable eastern hard rock sugar maple is the best for use in butcher block; it resists damage from cutting, scratching, warping, and uneven wearing. Though they're not quite as strong and will scratch more easily, western maple and western alder are other types suitable for use as a countertop material according to the NKBA, and they're slightly cheaper.

Your decision to use wood, even as a section of the countertop, requires a commitment to keep it sealed. In addition, given concerns about bacteria, you'll have to scrub the wood with antibacterial soap after exposing it to uncooked foods. If you select a wood countertop and maintain it properly you can expect it to last for more than 20 years.

STAINLESS STEEL

Many of today's kitchens feature lots of metal, but they don't appear antiseptic or cold. That's largely because designers balance the look by introducing vibrant colors and other materials into the room, such as ceramic tile or wood. Stainless steel used for a countertop, whether it is for the entire counter or just a section of it, can look quite sophisticated, especially with a wood trim. What's practical about it is its capacity to take high heat without scorching, which makes it suitable as a landing strip for pots and pans straight from the cooktop. It is also impervious to water, so it's practical at the sink. On the negative side, stainless steel can be noisy to work on, and it will show smudges. Depending on the grade of the material, it may also be vulnerable to scrapes, stains, and corrosion. The higher the chromium and nickel content (and therefore the grade), the better. Also, look for a thick-gauge stainless steel that won't dent easily. If you buy quality and care for it properly, a stainless-steel countertop should last at least 15 years.

FLOORING

As with every other product you select for the kitchen, flooring plays a role in establishing style, but it affects function, too. Generally, a material that is hard, such as stone or ceramic tile, can be uncomfortable to stand on for long periods of time. Resilient flooring and wood are more comfortable because they are more flexible than the others, having a bit of play in them. Therefore, consider your cooking style when selecting a flooring material for the kitchen. If you prepare long, complex menus, you'll be on your feet for extended periods of time, so always choose comfort over style.

Maintenance is another factor that should affect your decision about flooring. You'll have to weigh the different types, their aesthetic and practical values, for yourself. Here's what you should know before you do your comparison shopping.

WOOD

The varieties of wood available as a flooring surface are vast, and the cost varies widely, depending on the type and grade of the wood and the choice of design—whether it will be strips or parquet.

Softwoods, such as pine and fir, are often used to make simple tongue-and-groove floor boards. Softwoods are usually less expensive than hardwoods, but they're also less durable and aren't suited for high-traffic areas, rooms with heavy furniture that can "dig" into the wood, or for surfaces in rooms where chairs or other furniture will be moved around frequently. The hardwoods—maple, birch, oak, or ash—are much less likely to mar with normal use, but hardwoods are far from indestructible; they will stand up to use, but not abuse.

Color stains—reds, blues, and greens—may be appropriate in some kitchens, where a country or rustic feeling is desired. However, wood flooring is most often used to convey tone and feeling rather than a surface that brings

Opposite: *Stainless steel makes an ideal countertop material on this kitchen island designed for two cooks and with separate burners at each end. The metal surface easily takes the heat of hot pots and pans.*

Left: *A wood floor featuring a stenciled rug around the breakfast counter adds homespun charm to a country kitchen.*

Below: *A vintage tile pattern brings color into this room.*

color to a room. Natural wood stains range from the light ash tones to a deep coffee color. Generally, the lighter stains make a room feel more informal, and darker, richer stains suggest an atmosphere that is more traditional and reserved. Also, lighter stains—as with lighter paint or tile colors—create a feeling of openness and make a kitchen look larger, whereas darker stains tend to create an intimate feeling and reduce the visual expanse of a large space. The choice, however, is simply a personal one.

Above: *This cushioned sheet-vinyl flooring stylishly resembles garden pavers. It's also easy to maintain, comfortable, and kind to fragile objects that have been dropped. Although it's comparatively affordable, a high-quality product could cost as much to install as a ceramic-tile floor.*

The pattern of a wood floor also allows a designer to set the desired atmosphere of an interior. For example, for an Old World look, strips may be laid in a herringbone pattern. Decorative inlay with either strips or parquet patterns can enhance richness and visual interest and can be used to frame activity areas in large kitchens that have multiple uses and work zones.

As for maintenance, if a wood floor is properly sealed with polyurethane, its upkeep consists of vacuum-cleaning or dust-mopping as needed. It's important to promptly clean up any gritty material that may be tracked in from outdoors, because sand or gravel can scratch or even gouge the surface of a wood floor. If you take good care of your wood floor it should remain handsome for a lifetime.

LAMINATE PRODUCTS

When your creative side says "wood" or "stone," but your practical side says, "not a good idea in this room," the compromise may be laminate flooring, which is made from paper impregnated with melamine, an organic resin that is bonded to a core of particleboard, fiberboard, or other wood by-products. Laminate flooring can be installed over virtually any subflooring, including wood and concrete, as well as other surface flooring, such as ceramic or vinyl tiles, vinyl and other sheet flooring, and even certain types of carpeting. Also known as "faux wood" or "faux stone," depending on the finish, laminate may provide the look you desire along with the practical aspects you and your family can live with. Laminate is particularly well suited to kitchens, where stain and scratch resistance and quick cleanup are desirable. Manufacturers of this type of flooring offer warranties against staining, scratching, cracking, and peeling for up to 15 years.

VINYL AND OTHER RESILIENT FLOORING

Resilient flooring is available in sheet or tile form and is made from a variety of materials, including linoleum, asphalt or asphalt combined with asbestos, and rubber. However, the most commonly used material in manufacturing today's resilient flooring is vinyl plastic.

The most attractive features of resilient flooring include its price (making it among the most economical flooring options), its track record for long-lived, durable service,

and its relatively easy maintenance. The variety of colors and patterns is vast, and as with tiles, the combinations of color and pattern are virtually limitless. You can find styles that resemble the look of more expensive flooring materials. Even the sheet form of resilient flooring can be customized with the use of inlay strips. You can design the pattern yourself or with help from a flooring specialist.

Cushioned sheet vinyl offers the most resilience. It has good stain resistance; it's comfortable and quiet underfoot; and many brands offer no-wax and never-wax finishes. All features are especially attractive if the floor in a kitchen gets lots of kid traffic. On the negative side, only the more expensive grades show an acceptable degree of resistance to nicking and denting, and although the range of available colors, patterns, and surface textures is great, sheet flooring isn't as flexible as vinyl tile when it comes to creating a customized look. On the plus side, sheet products are available in an array of patterns.

Regular sheet vinyl is less expensive than the cushioned types, but it carries the same disadvantages and is slightly less resilient. Except for the availability of no-wax finishes, a vinyl-tile floor is as stain resistant and as easy to maintain as sheet-vinyl products, but its resilience is fair at best. On the other hand, design possibilities are greater with vinyl tiles. You can expect a good-quality vinyl or resilient floor to last between 20 and 30 years.

CERAMIC TILE

Ceramic tile is an excellent choice for areas that are subjected to a lot of traffic and in rooms where resistance to moisture and stains is a factor (See "Countertop Materials," page 65.) These features—combined with the fact that maintenance involves a simple, inexpensive soap-and-water cleaning—have made ceramic tile a handsome, centuries-old tradition for kitchen flooring.

When shopping, look for tiles that are manufactured specifically for floor installation. Ones that are highly glazed, for example, are hazardous underfoot. Instead, choose soft-glazed versions. Ask the salesperson about the manufacturer's slip-resistance rating for the tile you are selecting, too. Unless the tile is handmade or imported, it's an affordable flooring choice that can last a lifetime.

When you are creating a flooring design, consider whether the other elements in the room allow for an intricate pattern in the colors your creativity dictates or, instead, you need to visually enlarge the space by choosing one light color as the dominant feature. Once that basic determination has been made, you can draw your design on a copy of your floor plan. You should also include a color sketch of the design on your sample board.

When assessing whether ceramic tile is the right surface for your plan, remember that long-lasting beauty, design versatility, and easy care are accompanied by some features that can make ceramic tile hard to live with: It's cold underfoot, noisy when someone walks across it in hard-soled shoes, and not at all resilient—expect the worst when something breakable falls on a tile floor.

Above: *The stonelike quality of these tiles adds a Continental flavor to this room. The pattern resembles a motif found in old stone villas around the Mediterranean.*

Opposite: *Less refined but equally appealing are the natural clay pavers in this kitchen. They are the perfect accompaniment to the provincial pine cabinetry.*

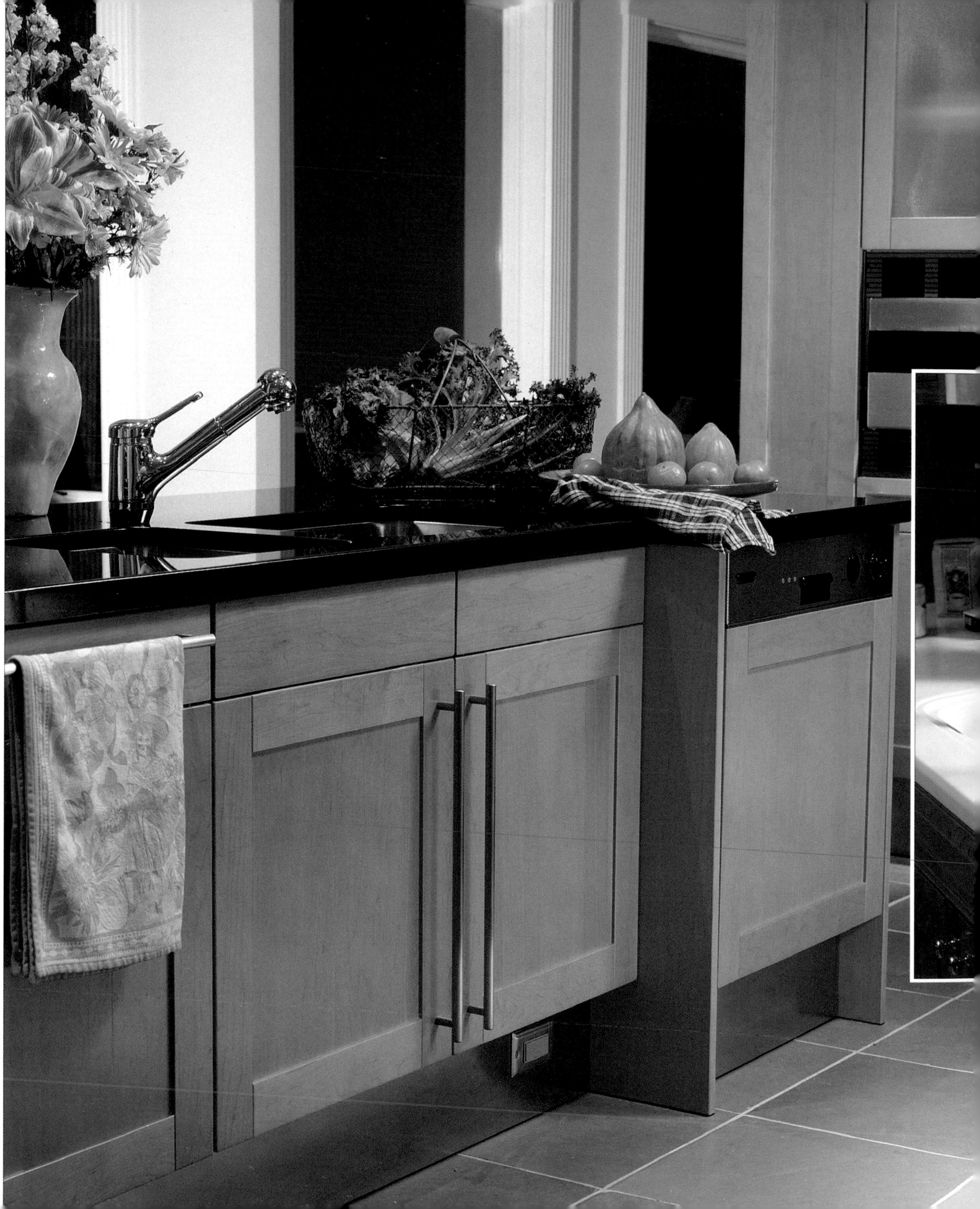

STONE AND CONCRETE

Along with ceramic tile, stone and concrete are among the flooring surfaces classified as "nonresilients." Like tile, properly sealed stone is unparalleled for durability, moisture- and stain-resistance, and ease of maintenance. It also shares with tile the drawbacks of being cold to the touch, noisy to walk on, and unforgivably hard—virtually guaranteeing that anything breakable that falls on a stone or concrete floor will not survive in one piece.

The comparison with tile ends, however, with some critically important features. On the plus side is the fact that these floors are clearly, unmistakably natural. As good as some faux surfaces look (and some are astonishingly good imitations, such as stone-look ceramic tiles), no product manufactured today actually matches the rustic irregularity of natural stone or the richness and depth of color in veined marble. The down side can be summed up in one word: cost. Whether it's slate, brick, concrete, limestone, sophisticated polished marble, or random-cut fieldstone, the material is expensive. However, it is durable and will last a lifetime. One caution: Find out whether you'll need additional support under the floor to carry the weight of the material.

FIXTURES

What could be more basic to the modern kitchen than a sink and faucet? Yet in today's world, there's practically nothing basic about them. Style comes in all price ranges, but high-performance technology is accompanied by an equally high price tag. There are designs and finishes to suit any contemporary or traditional tastes. And far from being just necessary items in a kitchen, sinks and faucets have evolved into highly decorative elements, as well. Here's what's on the market.

SINKS

These receptacles come in all sizes, shapes, and colors, and are typically fabricated from enameled cast iron, stainless steel, a composite material (solid-surfacing, acrylic, or a mixture of natural quartz or granite with resins), or solid stone. They may be hand-painted or decorated with silk-screened designs, contoured, beveled, brushed to a matte finish, or polished to a mirror finish. The trend is to include the largest sink that you can accommodate within the confines of your space. Deep bowls make it easier to deal with awkward oversized items, such as large roasting pans and tall pots used for cooking pasta, and they help to cut down on splashing. A good example is the farm-style (or exposed-apron) sink that, at one time, would have been regarded as *déclassé* but is reemerging in glamorous solid colors or with decorative patterns. Shallow-basin sinks are available when there is no other place to install the dishwasher but under the sink.

Opposite: *Concrete floor tiles resemble the cool look of natural slate. They complement designs such as this contemporary setting.*

Above: *An integral sink, countertop, and drainboard was fabricated from solid-surfacing material.*

Two- and three-bowl configurations are also gaining popularity. This arrangement allows you to separate clean dishes from dirty ones as well as from waste materials. Some sinks come with a colander and cutting board. Typically, a waste-disposal unit is installed with one of the bowls, usually the larger one. Just peel your potatoes, then whisk the skins down the drain. Lay the cutting board over the top of the bowl for chopping, and afterwards push the potato slices into the colander for rinsing. How's that for function?

Some designers recommend installing sinks in two separate areas. The primary sink often anchors the main food preparation and cleanup areas, while a smaller secondary sink serves outside of the major work zone. A second sink is a must when two or more people cook together routinely, but it is also handy if you practice crafts in the kitchen or entertain often and would use it as a wet bar. You can also use it as an extra place for washing hands when someone is using the main sink for preparing a meal.

Like every other kitchen product, there are numerous choices of sinks from which you will have to make a final selection, so it won't always be easy. In terms of durability, any one of the materials mentioned above will hold up well for years, if not decades, with the right care. Enameled cast-iron sinks tend to discolor but can be cleaned easily with a nonabrasive cleanser. Stainless steel and stone should be cleaned the same way. However, composite sinks are scratch resistant, with the exception of inexpensive acrylic models, so you can use an abrasive agent on them. Expect a quality sink to last as long as 30 years.

In terms of installation, there are five types of sinks for the kitchen to consider. They are:

☙ **Undermounted.** If you want a smooth look, an under-mounted sink may be for you. The bowl is attached underneath the countertop.

☙ **Integral.** As the word "integral" implies, the sink and countertop are fabricated from the same material—stone, faux stone, or solid-surfacing. There are no visible seams or joints in which food or debris can accumulate.

☙ **Self-rimming or flush-mounted.** A self-rimmed sink has a rolled edge that is mounted over the countertop.

☙ **Rimmed.** Unlike a self-rimming sink, this type requires a flat metal strip to seal the sink to the countertop.

☙ **Tile-in.** Used with a tiled countertop, the sink rim is flush with the tiled surface. Grout seals the sink to the surrounding countertop area.

FAUCETS

Faucets are no longer just conduits for water. From sleek European-inspired designs to graceful gooseneck shapes, today's selections add beauty as well as function to a kitchen. An excellent example is the pot-filler faucet, which

Below: *A wrist-blade handle is the easiest type to operate because you don't have to grasp the valve with your fist. Note the self-rimming edge of this stainless-steel sink.*

Opposite *A deck-mounted center-set faucet complements this copper sink. A pot-filler faucet has been installed on the wall above the commercial-style range.*

is mounted to the wall over the cooktop. Some versions have a pull-out spout; others come with a double- or triple-jointed arm that can be bent to reach up and down or swiveled back and forth, allowing the cook to pull the faucet all the way over to a pot on the farthest burner of a wide commercial range. Anyone who has ever had to lug a heavy pot of water from the tap to a burner will appreciate this convenience. Just remember: You'll need additional cold-water plumbing if you decide to install one of these faucets over your range or cooktop.

State-of-the-art technology in faucets gives you not only much more control over water use but better performance and finishes, as well. Features to look for include pull-out faucet heads, retractable sprayers, hot- and cold-water dispensing, single-lever control, antiscald and flow-control devices, a lowered lead content in brass components, and built-in water purifiers to enhance taste.

For a quality faucet, inquire about its parts when you shop. The best are those made of solid brass or a brass-base material. Both are corrosion-resistant. Avoid plastic components—they won't hold up. Ask about the faucet's valving, too. Buy a model that has a washerless cartridge; it will cost more, but it will last longer and be less prone to leaks. This will save you money in the long run.

Besides selecting a spout type (standard, arched, gooseneck, or pull-out), you may choose between single or double levers. Pull-out faucets come with a built-in sprayer if you want one. Others require installing a separate sprayer. Until recently, a pressure-balanced faucet (one equipped with a device that equalizes the hot and cold water coming out of a faucet to prevent scalding), came only with single-lever models. Now this safety feature is available with faucets that have separate hot- and cold-water valves. You may mix your spout with one of many types of handle styles: wrist blades, levers, scrolls, numerous geometric shapes, and cross handles. If your fingers or hands get stiff, choose wrist blades, which are the easiest to manipulate.

Chrome, brass, enamel-coated or baked-on colors, pewter, and nickel are typical faucet finishes. Make a fashion statement by mixing finishes or pair a matte, brushed, or antiqued look with one that is highly polished. Some finishes, such as chrome, are easier to care for than others; brass, for example, may require polishing. Always inquire about upkeep when you shop. Technologically advanced coatings can make even delicate finishes, like the enameled colors, more durable unless you use abrasive cleaners on them, which will scratch the finish. You may expect a good-quality faucet to last approximately 15 years; top-of-the-line products will hold up even longer.

In terms of installation, these are the three types of faucets to choose from:

❦ **Center set.** This faucet set features two separate valves, one for hot, the other for cold water, and a spout. However, all three pieces appear connected in one unit when they are installed.

Opposite: *An old-fashioned exposed-apron sink and back-mounted faucet with attached soap dish looks stylish in this refurbished kitchen.*

Right: *This reproduction faucet set in brass is paired with a matching hot-water dispenser.*

🐦 **Widespread.** This installation features a spout with two separate valves that appear to be three distinct pieces.

🐦 **Single lever.** This installation contains a spout and single lever in one piece for one-hand operation.

When you design your sink and faucet area, don't be side-tracked by the good looks of a product. Think about whether it works for your application. Today, good looks come in all types. Instead, compare the size of your biggest pots and racks to see whether the sink you're considering will accommodate them. If it won't and you can't install something deeper, pair the sink with a pull-out or goose-neck faucet. Always make sure it directs the flow of the water into the center of the bowl and slightly to one side. A spout that is proportionately too tall for the depth of the sink will splash water; one that is too short won't allow water to reach to the sink's corners. If you plan a double- or triple-bowl configuration, the spout should deliver water to each of the separate bowls.

MORE CONVENIENCES

While you're at it, you might consider installing a waste-disposal unit. (See Chapter Six, "Major Appliances & More.") It's a convenient way to get rid of food scraps, especially since many localities have to separate food from debris for recycling. New disposal units don't make that awful noise that older models do, so they're more pleasant to operate. To keep the unit smelling fresh, drop a lemon wedge down into it occasionally. Check with your building inspector before installing a disposal unit, however. Depending on where you live, it may be either mandated or outlawed by code. The lifespan of a waste-disposal unit is 10 years.

Another convenience you may want to include with your new sink and faucet is a hot- and cold-water dispenser. You can buy a unit that dispenses both, or just hot or cold water. These fixtures take up little space on the sink deck. Some are chrome; others come in colors, typically white. They operate via a small lever or push button. Some brands are part of a water-filtration system.

Right: *This kitchen epitomizes today's philosophy of mixed materials and varied worked surfaces.*

CABINETRY & STORAGE

Who can't relate to this scenario: You turn the oven on to preheat it, but wait, did you take out the large roasting pan first? How about the lasagna dish, muffin tins, pizza stone, and cookie sheets that are in there, too? Now where can you put everything that was in the oven while the casserole is baking and the countertop is laden with, among other things, vegetables and the rest of tonight's dinner ingredients?

The oven, it seems, has become the catchall for the big, awkward stuff that you can't fit into kitchen cabinets but is just too darn ugly to leave out. Besides, the countertop is where you keep the toaster oven, food processor, coffeemaker, canisters, hand mixer, portable TV, notepad, coupon file, bills, hand lotion, car keys, and your vitamins! Wouldn't life be grand if there was a place for everything and everything was in its place? Good cabinetry outfitted with an assortment of organizing options can help you there. It can make your kitchen more efficient and a whole lot neater while establishing a style, or "look," for the room. Keep in mind, however, that cabinetry will also consume about 40 percent of your remodeling budget, according to the NKBA. So before making any expensive decisions and, hopefully, no mistakes, investigate all of the various cabinetry options that are available to you.

Left: *Beautiful cabinetry will consume a sizable portion of your budget, but as this kitchen demonstrates, it goes a long way toward setting the style for a room, as well as organizing your storage needs.*

CABINET CONSTRUCTION

Basically, cabinets are constructed in one of two ways: *framed* or *frameless*. Framed cabinets have a traditional look, with a full frame across the face of the cabinet box that may show between closed doors. This secures adjacent cabinets and strengthens wider cabinet boxes with a center rail. Hinges on framed cabinets may or may not be visible around doors and drawers when they are closed. The door's face may be ornamented with raised or recessed panels, trimmed or framed panels, or a framed-glass panel with or without muntins (the narrow vertical and horizontal strips of wood that divide panes of glass).

Frameless cabinets—also known as European-style cabinets, although American manufacturers also make them—are built without a face frame and sport a clean, contemporary look. There's no trim or molding with this simple design.

Close-fitting doors cover the entire front of the box, no ornamentation appears on the face of the doors, and hinges are typically hidden inside the cabinet box.

Choosing one type over another is generally a matter of taste, although framed units offer *slightly* less interior space. But the quality of construction is a factor that always should be taken into consideration. How do you judge it? Solid wood is too expensive for most of today's budgets, but it might be used on just the doors and frames. More typical is plywood box construction, which offers good structural support, and solid wood on the doors and frames. To save money, cabinetmakers sometimes use strong plywood for support elements like the box and frame, and medium-density fiberboard for other parts like doors and drawer fronts. In yet another alternative, good quality laminate cabinets can be made with high-quality, thick particleboard underneath the laminate finish. The material will hold screws securely, and the cabinet won't warp over time.

There are other things to look for in cabinet construction. They include dovetail or mortise-and-tenon joinery and solidly mortised hinges. Also, make sure the interior of every cabinet is well finished, with adjustable shelves that are a minimum $5/8$ inch thick to prevent bowing.

MANUFACTURING STYLES

Unless you have the time and skill to build the cabinets yourself or can hire someone else to do it, you'll have to purchase them in one of four ways: *knockdown* (also known as RTA, or *ready to assemble*), *stock*, *semi-custom*, or *custom*. Prices vary from category to category, and even within each category. To make the wisest choice,

Left: *A framed cabinet door style and fine furniture details, such as molding and carved panels, create a traditional look in the kitchen.*

Opposite: *In a contemporary-style kitchen, an unframed door style and minimal decoration set the tone for the rest of the décor.*

be sure you know the differences that distinguish one type from another.

☙ *Custom cabinets* are not limited in terms of style or size because they are built to the designer's specifications. They are made from scratch, sometimes on-site or at the manufacturer, so they can take up to three months to be completed. The wait is worth it: These cabinets look like fine furniture in both their detailing and color. Of course, such craftsmanship isn't cheap. Custom cabinets can run in price from moderate to extremely expensive.

☙ *Semi-custom cabinets*, like custom ones, are made to measure, but by a large cabinet company at a price that is *usually* considerably lower than a local millwork shop would charge. This means they take about eight weeks to be delivered. As with all things, the cost will ultimately depend on quality, finish, and any extra features you order. Although styles and shapes are standard, semi-custom cabinets are produced to fit the homeowner's specific needs, which may include special sizes, interior organizers, and custom finishes.

☙ *Stock cabinets* are often available on the spot where they are sold or can be delivered quickly. Although they come in a great variety of standard sizes, making it easy for you to find what you need, they are limited in style and color. This means you can mix and match stock cabinets for a custom look, but you won't find a great selection from which to choose. However, you will find more interior features that only came with custom or semi-custom models not so long ago.

The quality of stock cabinets varies greatly by manufacturer and ranges from slightly below adequate to excellent. Inquire about what materials were used in the manufacture, the grade (quality) of the materials, and the type of joinery. Don't buy anything that is simply glued together—unless you plan to sell the house soon and just want to update the appearance of the kitchen to attract buyers.

☙ *Knockdown cabinets* are the most economical choice. They are basically stock cabinets that are shipped flat,

sometimes, and unfinished. The cost savings are realized because you put the pieces together yourself, and you stain or paint and install the cabinets yourself, too. The variety of styles is limited but current, and you can add personality with a special finish and interesting hardware. You don't have to be particularly handy to put together knockdown cabinets using a screwdriver and wrench, but you do have to invest the time in their assembly. This is a sensible choice if you are on a tight budget or you don't want to invest too much money in a kitchen renovation.

CABINET ACCESSORIES AND OPTIONS

Most people would agree that no matter how much storage space they have, they need even more. The problem often isn't the amount, it's the inaccessible placement and inefficient configuration of the storage space. One of the greatest benefits today's designers and manufacturers offer is fitted and accessorized interiors that maximize even the smallest

nook and cranny inside cabinets and drawers. These accommodations not only expand the use of space but increase convenience and accessibility. Among them are:

Appliance Garages. Appliance garages make use of dead space in a corner, but they can be installed anywhere in the vertical space between wall-mounted cabinets and the countertop. A tambour (rolltop) door hides small appliances like a food processor or anything else you want within reach but hidden from view. This form of mini-cabinet can be equipped with an electrical outlet and can even be divided into separate sections to store more than one item. Reserve part of the appliance garage for cookbook storage, or outfit it with small drawers for little items or spices. Customize an appliance garage any way you like.

Lazy Susans and Carousel Shelves. These rotating shelves maximize dead corner storage and put items like dishes or pots and pans within easy reach. A Lazy Susan rotates 360 degrees, so just spin it to find what you're looking for. Carousel shelves, which attach to two right-angled doors, rotate 270 degrees; open the doors and the shelves, which are actually attached to the doors, put any item within hand reach. Pivoting shelves are a variation on the carousel design and may or may not be door-mounted. In addition, units may be built into taller cabinets, creating a pantry that can store a lot in a small amount of space.

Fold-Down Mixer Shelf. This spring-loaded shelf swings up and out of a base cabinet for use, then folds down and back into the cabinet when the mixer is no longer needed.

Slide-Outs and Tilt-Outs. Installed in base cabinets, slide-out trays and racks store small appliances, linens, cans, or boxed items, while slide-out bins are good for holding onions, potatoes, grains, pet food, or potting soil—even garbage or recycling containers. A tilt-out tray is located in the often-wasted area just below the lip of the countertop in front of the sink and above base cabinet doors. It looks like a drawer but tilts open to provide a neat nook for sponges and scouring pads that tend to look messy when left on the counter or sink deck.

Opposite, top: *A small area can hold—and hide—a lot. This cabinet's counter flips up and the door opens to reveal storage for bottled water, drawer bins for potatoes and onions, and the garbage can. There's even a rack on the backside of the door for hanging awkward-sized cooking utensils.*

Opposite, bottom: *Slide-outs hold a large cookbook collection and odd items like serving baskets.*

Above, left: *A compartmentalized appliance garage makes room for a coffeemaker and carafe.*

Above: *Knife storage inside a wooden countertop is handy when chopping and slicing.*

Left: *Small appliance parts and canisters are kept in outfitted drawers so the countertop remains clear.*

Built-in Pantry Units. These fold-out or slide-out units can be fitted into narrow areas that might otherwise remain wasted. Store dry or canned goods here.

In addition to these options, check out everything a cabinet manufacturer has to offer to make the most of a cabinet's storage capacity. Other items to look for include special racks for trays and cookie sheets; drawer inserts for organizing spices and utensils, watertight recycling bins, wine racks, fold-down recipe book rests, sliding pot racks, built-in canister drawers, and plate racks.

THE DECORATIVE ROLE OF CABINETS
The look you create in your kitchen will be largely influenced by the cabinetry you select. Finding a style that suits you and how you will use your new kitchen is similar to

shopping for furniture. In fact, don't be surprised to see many fine furniture details dressing up the cabinets on view in showrooms and home centers today.

Besides architectural elements like fluted pilasters, corbels, moldings, and bull's-eye panels, look for details like fretwork, rope motifs, gingerbread trim, balusters, composition ornamentation (it looks like carving), even footed cabinets that mimic separate furniture pieces. If your taste runs toward less fussy design, you'll also find handsome door and drawer styles that feature minimal decoration, if any.

Woods and finishes are just as varied, and range from informal looks in birch, oak, ash, and maple to rich mahogany and cherry. Laminate finishes, though less popular than they were a decade ago, haven't completely disappeared from the marketplace, but color has been added to the once-ubiquitous palette of almond and white finishes.

Color is coming on strong on wood cabinetry, too. Accents in one, two, or more hues are pairing with natural wood tones. White-painted cabinets take on a warmer glow with tinted shades of this always popular neutral. Special "vintage" fin-

Opposite and below: *Fresh, vibrant hues energize this kitchen and add lots of visual interest to a large expanse of wood cabinetry. An exuberant tile backsplash ties the look together by repeating all of the colors of the kitchen's surfaces. Whimsical hardware adds a playful accent.*

Left: *This compact kitchen makes the most of its U-shaped arrangement of cabinetry.*

Above: *Pull-out counters at strategic areas, such as near the microwave, make convenient landing spots for hot dishes.*

Opposite, left and right: *Slide-outs installed in otherwise wasted space in base cabinets are outfitted to house spices next to the cooktop or with racks for linen towels.*

ishes, such as translucent color glazes, continue to grow in popularity, as do distressed finishing techniques such as wire brushing and rubbed-through color that add both another dimension and the appeal of handcraftmanship, even on mass-produced items. Contemporary kitchens, which histori-cally favor an all-white palette, are warming up with earthier neutral shades or less sterile off-whites.

If you're shy about using color on such a high-ticket item as cabinetry, try it as an accent on molding, door trim, or on the island cabinetry. Just as matched furniture suites have become passé in other rooms of the house, the same is true for the kitchen, where mixing motifs or creating an unfitted look can add sophistication and visual interest.

Designers use the warmth of wood and the personality of color to balance the high-tech look of commercial-style equipment, which is finding its way more and more into residential design (see Chapter Six: "Major Appliances and More"). Homeowners want their kitchens to work harder,

but they don't want them to look industrial, especially when open to other living areas of the home. Rather than appearing incongruous, this blending of traditional and commercial materials is surprisingly appealing.

HARDWARE

Another way to emphasize your kitchen's decorative style is with hardware. From exquisite reproductions in brass, pewter, wrought iron, or ceramic to handsome bronze, chrome, nickel, glass, steel, plastic, rubber, wood, or stone creations, a smorgasbord of shapes and designs is available. Some pieces are highly polished; others are matte-finished, smooth, or hammered. Some are abstract or geometrical; others are simple, elegant shapes. Whimsical designs take on the forms of animals or teapots, vegetables or flowers. Even just one or two great-looking door or drawer pulls can punch up a kitchen that may be lacking personality. Like mixing cabinet finishes, a combination of two hardware styles—perhaps picked up from other materials in the room—makes a big design statement. As the famed architect Mies Van der Rohe once stated, "God is in the detail." The most perfect detail in your new kitchen may be the artistic hardware you select.

Besides looks, consider the function of a pull or knob. You have to be able to grip it easily and comfortably. If your fingers or hands get stiff easily or if you have arthritis, select C- or U-shaped pulls. If you like a knob, try it out in the showroom to make sure it isn't slippery or awkward when you grab it. Knobs and pulls can be inexpensive if you can stick to unfinished ones that you can paint in an accent color picked up from the tile or wallpaper. If you don't plan to buy new cabinets, changing the hardware on old ones can redefine their style. The right knob or pull can suggest any one of a number of vintage looks or decorative styles from Colonial to Arts and Crafts to Postmodern. (For suggestions about the right hardware for your cabinets, see Chapter Eight: "Adding Personality to Your Kitchen.")

PLANNING YOUR STORAGE

Now that you know that there are cabinets and accessories that make the most disorganized person's kitchen a model of neatness and efficiency, a thoughtful approach to planning storage for the new design is in order. The time to do this is *before* plans are on paper or work has begun. Here are a few ideas to get you started.

ONE: *Analyze your needs.* Make a detailed list of your shopping and cooking habits. How do you buy food? If you buy in bulk, how much of it has to be stored in the refrigerator? Do you need special storage for wines or bottled vinegars? A lot of canned goods, boxed grains, and pasta will need cabinet space. The NKBA conducted a study several years ago that revealed that most kitchens regularly store 18 cans of vegetables, 23 spices, and six boxes of cereal. How does yours compare?

Think about your cooking and serving utensils. Where are you most likely to use them? In the preparation area? By the cooktop? In both places? If you frequently use a wok or other typically awkward items, you might want to design special compartments or open shelves that keep them handy but hidden when not in use. The NKBA study says that most kitchens house 791 pots, pans, and dishes. (That includes glassware and china.) Are most of your utensils presently contained in the kitchen? Would you like to add the storage to do so?

Are your smaller appliances, such as a mixer and food processor, hand-held or larger? Are they heavy or awkward to move? If so, including an appliance garage in your design makes sense if you use these items often.

Somehow the kitchen is the catchall for many noncooking- and noneating-related items, too. If you don't think that will change once your new kitchen is completed, prepare for it. If, for example, your craft supplies, gardening tools, outdoor grilling items, and cleaning supplies are now stored on the countertop or on top of the refrigerator, reserve space for them on your formal plan—either inside a cabinet, in the pantry, or on shelves.

TWO: *Install cabinet accessories.* The specialized storage options detailed earlier can be a little pricey, but they are less expensive if you purchase them with your cabinetry. Adding them later or retrofitting them into older cabinetry can boost the cost even higher. If funds are restricted, perhaps you could limit them to a few.

There are other accessories that can keep items neatly organized when cabinet space is at a premium. Besides the ubiquitous wire shelf and bin options, a wall- or ceiling-mounted

Bottom, left: *Some solutions to cabinet organization are simple. In this case, the homeowner simply used a wooden plate rack that can be purchased in the housewares section of a department store or a kitchen speciality shop.*

Below, right: *Open-shelf storage can be quite charming in the right setting, particularly in an informal country-style kitchen. Baskets, crockery, or even a tin pail can be useful, as well as part of the display.*

Opposite, left: *Outfitting a deep drawer with several compartments to separate different types of refuse makes recycling easy.*

Opposite, right: *A colorful collection of vintage Fiestaware looks decorative stored behind glass-door cabinets.*

pot rack can make use of otherwise overlooked overhead space. A knife rack that attaches to the wall or the outside of a cabinet is also handy. Wall racks that hold wine, barware, spices, mops and brooms, and ironing boards are negligible in price, but invaluable space savers.

THREE: *Compartmentalize.* Make a plan *now* to store like things together, and tailor your shelf heights to these needs. Group utensils, pots, and pans by size. Group foods by type. Not only will this maximize the use of space, it will make finding what you need easier.

FOUR: *Plan to recycle.* Don't make recycling an afterthought. If you don't want to run outdoors to the various recycling receptacles, try to incorporate a place in the kitchen to separate them unobtrusively. Slide-out bins are an excellent solution if you can spare the cabinet space. In some kitchens a slide-out can accommodate two containers: The one in front is reserved for nonrecyclables; the second container is solely for recyclable trash.

FIVE: *Be honest about your habits.* If you're not a particularly neat person, avoid open shelving. The same advice applies to glass-fronted cabinets. Use just one or two of these cabinets for an attractive display.

Now that you have analyzed both your kitchen lifestyle and cooking style, you're ready to move on. The *honest* evaluation of your wants, needs, and preferences has prepared you to deal with the next big question—what about appliances?

MAJOR APPLIANCES & MORE

You may be intrigued, perhaps even dazzled, by all the choices in major appliances. With such a variety, it's important to analyze your needs carefully during the planning stages of any project, not when you get to the showroom and a salesperson woos you with an appliance's high-tech delights. That isn't to say that state-of-the-art equipment and optional features aren't worth your consideration. Indeed, most of them are intended to improve the efficient use of time spent in the kitchen. But new appliances will consume a considerable portion of your remodeling budget, so you've got to choose wisely. Whatever you decide on will be something you'll live with every day for quite a while; most ranges, cook-tops, and wall ovens will last as long as 15 to 20 years. The way to get the most for your money is to purchase the model and size that's right for your lifestyle now—and for the not-too-distant future.

When you shop, always remember: The equipment you own should not determine what's for dinner. Rather, whoever does the cooking should decide what kind of equipment he or she requires. Thankfully, manufacturers and technology now make it possible to custom-equip a kitchen with the types of general and special appliances that cater to the tastes and habits of both cook and family. This chapter describes your choices in major appliances, including cooking appliances, refrigerators, and dishwashers; plus not-so-major but definitely helpful, related items, such as

Left: *Commercial appliances, as well as commercial-style models, are making their way into residential design today. They're admired as much for their looks as for their performance.*

microwave ovens, range hoods and down-draft ventilators, waste-disposal units, and trash compactors. The chapter also talks about the bells and whistles that can raise the job of preparing a meal to a fine art—including commercial appliances—and whether that investment is really wise for you.

COOKERS

There are two basic questions you'll have to answer up front about your cooking equipment. What kind of fuel does it use, gas or electric, and will it be a configuration of separate burner and oven units or will it be contained in one unit?

If you can't make up your mind about fuel, you should at least know that the type you select makes a difference. After reviewing the advantages and disadvantages of each, you may want to combine both types into your plans.

Should you install a range or separate burners and ovens? The range is a smart choice if you have limited space. It may also be the most economical option because you won't incur the cost of multiple hookups and additional ventilation. However, it's not the best choice when more than one cook will work in the kitchen at the same time. And let's face it, when you're stirring the pot on top of the stove while roasting something in the oven, the heat buildup can become uncomfortable if not unbearable.

RANGES

You generally have a choice between a free-standing range, a slide-in model that fits between two base cabinets and sits on the floor, or a drop-in version, which is installed between two cabinets and must be fastened to the side of each of them. A drop-in range needs a base, which is normally constructed of wood. Drop-ins can hang from the countertop or sit on a low cabinet base. They are usually installed with a matching cabinet panel under them to provide storage. Drop-ins offer an economical approach to a built-in custom look, with minimal space required. Both the slide-in and drop-in models are designed to look built-in: The controls are placed in front so they can be used in islands or peninsulas as well as in a straight run of wall cabinetry.

Left: *A French import,* La Cornue *is a range that offers sophisticated technology with Old World charm. A major investment, it's a stove you'll take with you if you move.*

Opposite: *Gas is still the fuel of choice for serious cooks. A modular cooktop offers the most flexibility in terms of design and installation.*

If you are replacing your old range with a new one that has to fit into a preexisting opening, measure the front of the old unit. The typical size is 30 inches wide, although you can find both narrower and wider models. Extras to look for in a new range include interchangeable modular elements such as a drop-in wok, a grill or griddle, an oversize burner for large pots, a warming drawer, and a self-cleaning oven. Of course, the more features, the higher the price.

SEPARATE COOKTOPS AND OVENS

Separate cooktops and wall ovens are convenient if you have the room. This arrangement allows you to customize the work centers and install them where they fit best into the traffic pattern and work flow. It is ideal in a kitchen with multiple cooks. Modular units let you tailor your cooking system to the way you cook. Besides two-, four-, five-, six-, or eight-burner units, you can purchase accessories—built-in units or detachable, interchangeable parts for greater flexibility and easy cleanup. If you can afford the cost of adding extra ventilation and want to create even more convenience for two cooks, install four or six burners in one part of the work area and an additional pair elsewhere.

Another practical device is a warming drawer; models made for the residential market are built-in. You can purchase a commercial unit, which can be freestanding or built-in, but it carries a higher price tag. Either version measures 24 or 27 inches. Most manufacturers make warming drawers to match other appliances in their lines, but you can outfit them with a trim finish that blends with the cabinetry, as well. Look for a model with an adjustable setting that ranges from *crisp* to *moist* and comes with flexible racks.

COOKIN' WITH GAS

The bottom line is: You need heat—and lots of it. But you must to be able to control it and adjust it easily and quickly. In that department, gas delivers, which is why professional chefs prefer it. For better, quicker cooking results, burners have to produce at least 15,000 Btu (British thermal units, the measurement for heat output), but gas burners manufactured for the residential market typically deliver 30 to 50 percent less than that amount. That's why you can never prepare a steak at home that tastes quite as good as one that has been prepared in a restaurant. You can't raise the flame high enough to sear the meat properly.

Should you buy a commercial range? Probably not. The tremendous heat it generates will increase the risk of fire and injury in your home. Codes for installing this type of range are strict—some areas even prohibit the installation of commercial equipment. A commercial range also requires special venting and minimum clearances between it and adjacent cabinets or combustible materials or surfaces. However, you may want to consider a commercial-*style* range, which will allow you to set flames as high as 15,000 Btu and to bring them down to 360 Btu (on some models) for low simmering. Some units come with the option of one high-flame burner (12,000 to 15,000 Btu) in addition to regular burners and a larger-than-standard capacity oven.

If you think gas cooktops are difficult to keep clean, new sealed gas burners may be the answer because the cooking surface is extended around the heating element. No more drip plates and no more escaping flames. In addition, some gas cooktops come equipped with electronic ignition; some models will automatically reignite if a pot boils over and extinguishes the flame—that's a smart safety feature.

You can adjust the flame, use any size pot, and cook more evenly on a gas burner, it's true. If you want to switch from electric to gas service, you'll need to run a gas line into the kitchen besides buying the new appliance. First check with the building department in your area, and then speak to a plumber who can install and route the pipe. The price of the job depends on the complexity of your situation. A free estimate is always worth the time it takes.

For the look and charm of an old-fashioned cast-iron stove, you might consider an English import, the AGA cooker, which uses natural gas or propane to create the radiant heat

of a wood- or coal-burning type. (Authentic wood- or coal-burning models are also available.) This is an heirloom-quality appliance with a cooktop that features a warming plate, boiling plate, and simmering plate. Insulating lids cover the latter elements when they are not in use. Some models have four ovens for baking, roasting, warming, and simmering, but a two-oven cooker is also available. The AGA can be vented through a flue to the outdoors; a down-draft type of vent is also available and allows placement of the cooker anywhere in the room.

If this appeals to you, you should know that an AGA cooker has to stay on all the time because it takes hours to heat up, but it is energy efficient. Still, if you live in a warm climate or don't have air conditioning, you may find that it makes the kitchen stuffy. On the other hand, there is a new model that features standard gas burners and two electric ovens. An AGA cooker usually costs about ten times more than what you'll pay for a standard gas range—so check your bottom line before planning your design around it.

Right: *The English AGA cooker, paired here with a small standard range, brings the appeal of an old-fashioned cast-iron stove to the kitchen.*

Opposite: *Commercial-style ranges manufactured for the residential market often feature additional burners, including at least one that heats up to 15,000 Btu, plus a grill or griddle.*

Francophiles, the French *La Cornue* stove has similar visual appeal and a bit more technology. Some models feature a combination of high- to low-heat gas and electric burners for cooking up-to-the-minute, versatile capability.

ELECTRIC COOKTOPS

Despite the virtues of gas fuel, some people feel more comfortable with electric burners because they don't like the idea of an exposed flame or the cleaning required by standard gas burners. If that's your preference, you should know that watts are to electric cooktops what Btu is to gas-powered models. The more wattage, the quicker-cooking the cooktop. There are several kinds to consider.

Coil Elements. These are the traditional electric cooking surfaces—and the least expensive. Using conduction and radiation, they heat up quickly but take time cooling, so you can't go from sizzle to simmer instantly as you can with gas. And although you can use a wide variety of cookware with electric burners, pans must have flat bottoms and extend no more than 2 inches beyond the heating element for optimal results.

Ceramic glass. Also called *radiant-heat cooking surfaces*, this type features electric coils directly under translucent glass, which transfers heat more efficiently to the cookware than older, opaque, white ceramic surfaces.

It also uses higher-wattage heating elements. The smooth, sleek appearance of ceramic glass cooktops appeals to contemporary tastes. The finish is scratch- and stain-resistant, but it can be damaged by abrasive cleansers. You'll need flat-bottomed, heavy-gauge metal pans to heat food quickly and effectively with ceramic glass, and cookware should not extend more than 1 inch beyond the cooking area.

Smart Tip about Commercial-Style Ranges

Don't assume that a commercial-*style* range is the same as a "professional-style" unit. Professional style usually means the appliance is finished in stainless steel so it *looks* like a commercial model. This is fine if you like the appearance of commercial equipment, and that's the only reason you're buying it. But if you want more power, choose commercial-style. To be on the safe side, ask the dealer or salesperson about the Btu level of the burners in the model *before* you buy it.

Right: *There are several types of electric cooktops available today. This one features traditional electric coils. Some people prefer electric to gas for safety reasons, but you can burn yourself on a coil even after it's been turned off because it takes time to cool down.*

Opposite: *An induction cooktop always stays cool to the touch—only the cookware heats up.*

Below the surface, the coils produce a high-frequency alternating magnetic field that flows through the cookware. Most of the heat on the cooktop is absorbed by the pan. Without a pan or utensil, the heating coil is de-energized and turns itself off. Induction cooktops require magnetic-responsive cookware, which means pots and pans for use with this appliance must be steel, porcelain-on-steel, stainless steel, or cast iron.

Manufacturers of induction cooktops boast of its quick response—it can go from high heat to low heat instantly—and the precise temperature control.

OVENS

An oven has to be well insulated to bake evenly and broil foods adequately. Again, fuel is an important factor. Many professional chefs prefer electric ovens because they brown food more uniformly than gas models. Broiling, however, is done best at a high temperature, which would tend to recommend gas. Designers often specify two ovens for layouts that can accommodate more than one work triangle. (See Chapter Two: "Creating Functional Space.") If two ovens can work in your plan, you could install one powered by gas for broiling, while reserving the electric oven for baking. If you have only enough room for a range, you can buy a dual-fuel model—gas burners and an electric oven.

Halogen. Similar to ceramic glass cooktops, especially with regard to cookware and cleaning, halogen units combine resistant heating wires and halogen lamps that are located beneath a ceramic-glass cover to create heat.

Induction. This ceramic-glass cooking surface uses electro-magnetic energy to heat the cookware, not the cooktop, making it safe because no heat is generated by a flame or coil. An induction cooktop is also easy to keep clean; because the surface remains relatively cool, spills don't burn and turn into a crusty mess that requires scrubbing.

Size is another consideration. An oven with extra capacity will cost more, but it's definitely an advantage. Kitchen designers are increasingly recommending 27- and 30-inch models over the standard 24-inch versions. If you really need it, a 36-inch model is available. As a frame of reference when making up your mind regarding the size you need, remember: You can roast a 20-pound turkey nicely in a standard-size oven.

Wall ovens are the easiest and safest to use when they are installed at waist height. If you can afford a pair of ovens, don't install them one above the other; either the bottom one will require awkward bending, or the top unit will be too high for safely transferring food. Ideally, two wall ovens should be placed side by side or located in different work areas.

For ease of maintenance, shop for a self-cleaning model. The cleaning systems of electric ovens are more effective than those of gas-powered units because of their even heat distribution. Also, poke your head into the cavity of any oven you're considering; dark interiors retain heat and hide grime better than light ones. Test the racks. Are they easy to maneuver yet secure in place? Is the light bulb accessible for changing it? Is it bright enough? Digital clocks and timers; preset options for baking, cleaning, timing, and temperature settings; and push-button temperature controls are some of the extra features you can have with a new oven— at an additional price.

Convection Ovens. You may want to consider one of these as a *second* oven, if only because it can't broil (the heating source is located outside the cavity). It works like this: The oven circulates heated air around the food, pulls the air out of the cooking cavity, reheats the air over a hot element, and returns the reheated air to the cavity. It does have a drying effect, so you don't want to cook foods in a convection oven that should retain lots of moisture, but it's terrific for baking pastry or roasting chicken because it makes outer layers crisp. Other advantages to a convection oven include its ability to bake or roast faster than a conventional model, at temperatures that are 25 to 75 degrees Fahrenheit lower, which saves energy. And because superheating the air over hot elements burns off odors, it's possible to bake dissimilar foods, such as pound

Opposite: *Though it's not uncommon to stack two wall ovens, the arrangement will mean extra bending or reaching.*

Above: *A convection oven is an ideal second oven in a kitchen, particularly if you do a lot of baking, because it bakes evenly.*

cake and pizza, at the same time. There are some multiple-mode models on the market that can switch from conventional- to convection- to microwave-oven cooking, although they are considerably more expensive than standard models, but perhaps not more than the cost of all three combined.

Microwave Ovens. Microwave units cut down cooking time for some foods to mere minutes, with more powerful models (750 to 1,000 watts) cooking faster. But roasts don't brown, and meat, fish, and fowl must be covered for at least part of the cooking time to prevent overcooking. Microwave-oven cookware should be mostly nonmetallic—anything ceramic, most plastics, and paper—because dishes or pans with a metal coating or trim may cause arcing.

However, microwave ovens also have their advantages. They defrost and reheat foods quickly and efficiently, which is great for busy families. A model with an extra shelf lets you

Opposite: *Locate a microwave at eye level so you can watch what's cooking. Besides, reaching for a hot dish or casserole can be dangerous.*

Left: *A ducted ventilation system with a range hood is the most efficient type you can install.*

addition to the type of cooking appliances and the cost of any optional features you purchase, factor in the potential price of replacing any or all of your cookware. Again, let your lifestyle and cooking style lead your way.

VENTILATION

No discussion of cooking equipment is complete without addressing ventilation. The grease, smoke, heat, and steam generated when you cook will take their toll on your new cabinets, countertops, floors, walls, and other surfaces, where they collect along with germs and general grime. The only efficient way to combat this residue and the stale cooking odors that linger is with an exhaust system. A fan over the range or cooktop is not enough. The most effective way to ventilate a kitchen is with a hooded system. The hood, which is installed directly over the cooking surface, captures the bad air as it heats and naturally rises. A fan expels the contaminants to the outside through a duct. A damper inside the hood closes when the system is turned off so that cold air can't enter the house from the outside. Don't try to save money by installing a ductless fan: Any system that isn't ducted to the outside is useless.

reheat more than one dish at a time, and ones equipped with sensors can tell when some foods are done by the amount of steam or humidity they produce during cooking. Temperature-sensitive devices can be preset to reduce heat from a cooking to a warming level once the food gets hot enough. Another program allows you to indicate the weight of the food item, then rely on the microwave to decide how long to cook it and the appropriate heat level. Installation on or under a shelf that's at eye level makes it easy to monitor microwave cooking, but a countertop installation is also fine. Place a microwave near the refrigerator if you'll use it often to prepare frozen food or to reheat cold meals, or locate it in a secondary work zone so that the kids can make snacks without getting in your way. Remember: In

Although handsome hoods can create a focal point in the kitchen, most people don't regard ventilation as a glamorous feature. However, it is one of the most important— not only for preserving the good looks of your new room but for your safety and health. When installing a range hood, keep in mind that manufacturers recommend a maximum distance of 21 to 30 inches between the cooktop and the bottom of the hood in order to get the best ventilation. The hood should also be slightly longer and wider than the cooking surface.

An alternative to a system that uses a hood is down-draft ventilation, which is often installed in conjunction with an island cooktop or grill. The vent is in the countertop and the fan is below it. Down-draft venting works by forcing the air

above the burners through a filter, then moving it out of the house via ductwork that runs to the outdoors. This method is not as effective as a hooded system, but it is more effective than a ductless fan. Both hooded and nonhooded systems require a powerful fan. The more cooking you do, the more power you need—especially if you use high heat often

Opposite: *Though design glamour doesn't come to mind in a discussion of range hoods, it does appear to be the case in this handsome example.*

Above: *A down-draft vent is located on the countertop behind the burners of this cooktop. Sometimes the vent is situated on the counter between the burners.*

(stir frying, for example). Check the air-movement rating of the fan for your unit (given in cubic feet per minute, or cfm). The NKBA recommends a minimum of 150 cfm per linear foot for cooktops or ranges installed against a wall and 180 cfm per linear foot for cooktops or grills installed in an island. Commercial-style equipment requires a fan with a 1,200 to 1,800 cfm rating because the heat it generates is higher. Also, long runs of ductwork necessitate a fan with greater power. In general, keep ductwork as short as possible. Long, winding runs of ductwork require more powerful fans. Calculating specific needs can be complicated in these situations, so consult your contractor.

REFRIGERATORS & FREEZERS

A refrigerator/freezer has a life expectancy of about 15 years, so if yours is approaching that mark or if it is more than 10 years old, you'd be wise to replace it. Today's more-efficient models can save up to 50 percent more energy than ones made in the early 1980s. And not only will a new refrigerator save energy, it will also provide better storage with flexible interior space that can be reconfigured and tailored to your needs. Shelves move up and down easily and extra-deep door bins can even accommodate a gallon container.

Typical full-size refrigerators range from 8 to 30 cubic feet. What size is right for you? It depends on how many people live in your house. Conventional wisdom recommends allocating 12 cubic feet for two people in a household and another 2 cubic feet for each additional person. Increase the total by another 2 cubic feet if you entertain often. That's the formula, but not all lifestyles fit neatly into it. If you eat out more than once or twice a week or shop daily for food, you don't need that much storage. If you have teenage children, shop in bulk, buy large containers of soda, juice, and milk, and frequently require space for large party platters, you'll need a refrigerator that is roomy enough to accommodate these considerations.

Right: *A custom-made trim kit allows this refrigerator and its bottom-mounted freezer to blend in seamlessly with the rest of the kitchen cabinetry.*

Opposite: *Extra features, such as through-the-door ice and water and a drop-down shelf that allows access to items stored on the interior side of the door, can save energy.*

Above and below: *Modular refrigerator drawers allow point-of-use placement. They come in numerous finishes or with cabinet-coordinated trim kits.*

Your analysis should come down to common sense. If your family regularly eats fresh fruits and vegetables, a roomy crisper should be on your list of must-haves. If they eat cold meats and cheese, you'll want a separate drawer for those items. Do you precook meals for the week or buy frozen foods? If so, shop for a model with a generous freezer compartment. If you have extra-large freezing needs, consider buying an additional stand-alone freezer. As you make your selection, keep in mind that the fuller a refrigerator or freezer, the less it costs to run. So don't waste energy dollars with one that is too large for either your household or the amount of food you keep on hand. Keep any refrigerator at least two thirds full for maximum efficiency.

Refrigerator sizes vary by more than capacity. Traditionally, units have protruded beyond the full depth of a base cabinet. As kitchen design has become sleeker, manufacturers have responded with 24-inch-deep models that fit snugly into a corresponding-size opening in a run of cabinetry for a built-in appearance. (Refrigerators can be finished with trim kits or custom panels to match your cabinets.) But as refrigerators have become shallower, they have also become wider to make up for lost storage capacity. Width varies greatly, so check the appliance's spec sheet when you're allocating space on the layout. Most conventional refrigerators come in one of three styles with a freezer on top, with a freezer on the bottom, or with refrigerator and freezer side by side. There are also a number of optional features offered with today's refrigerators, including water-purifying systems with through-the-door water and ice, slide-out shelves, zoned temperature control, automatic ice makers, wine racks, front venting, see-through bins and adjustable drawers, wine caddies, door alarms, automatic defrosting, and on-the-door shelves and separate meat, cheese, and butter keepers.

Top-Mounted Freezer. The freezer compartment is on the top and is completely separate from the refrigerator. This is the most energy-efficient style because cold air from the freezer blows down into the refrigerator and helps cool that section. These may be available with an optional through-the-door ice and water dispenser.

Bottom-Mounted Freezer. This configuration locates a separate pullout freezer drawer below the refrigerator. Its style does not allow for a through-the-door ice and water

Left and below: *Side-by-side refrigerators typically don't interfere with traffic aisles because the doors are narrow, but they don't always accommodate oversized objects like pizzas and large platters.*

Opposite: *Custom-made trim panels keep the dishwasher relatively unobtrusive in this kitchen.*

at an island or peninsula that serves as a bar or buffet. The concept of modular refrigeration and freezer drawers is gaining popularity, making a logical argument for point-of-use storage and refrigeration in larger kitchens with multiple work triangles. Imagine keeping the vegetables in a refrigerated compartment right under the counter where you rinse and chop them. These modular units fit neatly under standard

dispenser, but it does put refrigerated foods at a more comfortable height; you don't have to bend to get to the fruit bin or to the bottom door shelves.

Deciding between a top- or bottom-mounted refrigerator depends on which section—freezer or refrigerator—you want to be more accessible.

Side-by-Side Refrigerator/Freezer. This style offers the greatest access to both compartments and requires the least door-swing clearance in front. However, unless you're installing a 48-inch-wide model, typically narrow shelves may not handle bulky items like a turkey or a frozen pizza. This style is usually available with an optional through-the-door ice and water dispenser and a drop-down shelf that allows you access to items stored inside on the door. Both features save energy because they cut down on opening the door.

Modular Refrigerators. Under-counter refrigerators may solve some design difficulties and provide storage for specialized needs, such as chilling soft beverages or wine

counters and come with drawer dividers and their own temperature-control devices, which let you make adjustments for vegetables, milk, and meat. If you're thinking about installing modular refrigeration, consult manufacturers' spec sheets for information on plumbing and electrical requirements.

COMMERCIAL REFRIGERATORS

You may like the way some commercial units look, with glass doors or an all stainless-steel appearance, but they really make no sense for residential use. If your family is like most, it spills and splashes its share of liquidy stuff inside the refrigerator. Can you live with that mess showing through a glass door? Do you have the time keep after it? On the other hand, if all you want is a stainless-steel finish, you can get it in a refrigerator designed in a standard size for residential use.

Besides paying more for the status-symbol satisfaction of owning an expensive commercial refrigerator, you'll also likely have a much higher energy bill. Commercial units are considerably larger than those designed for home use. And remember, a refrigerator must be well-stocked to be efficient. Can you keep a large unit filled with the quantity of food a restaurant must have on hand? A commercial refrigerator won't make your life easier. If you have the extra money in your remodeling budget for this expensive item, spend it on something that will.

NEAR-THE-SINK APPLIANCES

Many people would agree that preparing a meal can be creative, even fun. Cleaning up afterwards, however, is a lot less satisfying. Modern appliances have taken much of the drudgery out of that task, thankfully. Now, manufacturers have improved the technology involved, too.

DISHWASHERS

Several innovations have improved dishwashers in recent years. A good model that is 25 percent more energy

Smart Tip about Dishwashers

New quieter models owe their silence in large part to better insulation. If you can't afford the higher price of one that has this advantage, ask your contractor to add some cushioning between the outside walls of the dishwasher and the sides of the cabinets that flank it. This will absorb some of the noise.

efficient and uses less water than one manufactured in the early 1990s should cost only a few hundred dollars and will last about 10 years. If you're willing to pay double that price, you can get features that not only conserve more energy and water but reduce the noise the appliance makes to something just above a whisper. Also worth your consideration—and a higher price—is a unit with a stainless-steel interior, which can take the beating of dishwashing chemicals and high heat on a daily basis. It will last for 20 years or more.

Another optional feature that may interest you is convection drying, which uses a built-in fan to air-dry dishes instead of the energy-consuming heat cycle. For more energy savings, some dishwashers have an internal heating device, so you can turn down the setting on your water heater. You can also find modular units that allow you to wash fine glassware separately from pots and pans or wash a small load. Then there's concealed controls, custom front panels, a built-in water-softening feature, pot-washing and fine-china cycles, delayed-start mechanisms, rinse-and-hold and soak-and-scrub options, and adjustable racks that will accommodate oversized platters.

A standard size dishwasher can slide into a 24-inch-wide space under a standard 36-inch-high countertop. If space near the sink is skimpy, consider an under-sink model, which can be installed under the shallow bowl of a sink designed specifically for this purpose. There are 18-inch-wide dishwashers, but they don't hold much. However, you might be able to use one as a second dishwasher if you entertain often.

A portable model might be another option for anyone who can't sacrifice cabinet space but has the floor space.

WASTE-DISPOSAL UNITS

These convenient devices shred organic wastes and send them down the drain. Some communities require disposal units; others ban them. Check with your local building authority before deciding whether to install one.

A *continuous-feed disposal unit* allows you to feed waste into the mechanism as it operates. A *batch-feed unit* grinds up to $1^1/_2$ to 2 quarts at a time. Continuous-feed models are controlled by a wall switch, batch-feed models by a built-in switch activated by replacing the drain lid. Batch-feed models are safer to use, but more expensive. Local codes may dictate which type you can buy. Although waste-disposal units make a lot of noise, the newer models operate more quietly. The life expectancy is about 10 years.

Left: *A trash compactor located at a second sink keeps refuse away from the food preparation area and allows the homeowner to rinse off `tems intended for recycling.*

TRASH COMPACTORS

If you live in a community that charges by the bag for removing garbage, you'll appreciate the savings a trash compactor may offer.

Inside the appliance, a screw-driven ram compresses inorganic debris—cans or bottles, for example—to about 25 percent of their original volume. Compactors come in slide-out or drop-front models that range in size from 12 to 18 inches wide. Some models stand alone, but a well-planned kitchen can incorporate a compactor that is built-in and finished to match the cabinetry. Compactors don't use much electricity, but most require special heavy-duty bags. Extras you may want to consider include a fan, deodorizer, safety lock, and quiet motor. You can expect a trash compactor to last about 10 years.

HOT-WATER DISPENSERS

These handy devices heat $\frac{1}{3}$ or $\frac{1}{4}$ gallon of water at a time and hold it at a bubbling 190 degrees Fahrenheit—an ideal temperature for making tea, coffee, or soup. (See Chapter Four, "Shopping for Products & Materials.") While the main components fit under the sink, the dispenser tap may attach to the hole in the sink deck originally intended for the sprayer or through a hole in the countertop, with water lines running through any cabinet wall. The device's heating element requires access to an electrical line under the counter.

SHOPPING TIPS

Once you're ready to outfit your kitchen with new appliances, review the "Smart Steps" in Chapter Four: "Shopping for Products & Materials." Here are additional tips.

 ONE: *Make sure the appliance is simple to use.* Ask for an in-store demonstration. You want the appliance to perform with space-age precision, but you shouldn't have to be an aeronautical engineer to use it. Also, check knobs and key pads. They should be within convenient reaching distance (on the front or side of the appliance) and easy to read, and they should accommodate any finger size—from a teenager's to an adult man's.

TWO: *Buy something that's easy to keep clean.* You want to enjoy the new kitchen, but you won't if it's drudgery to keep it sparkling. Inquire about the finish and care—inside and out—of every appliance you purchase. For example, a stainless-steel finish on the exterior of an appliance tends to show fingerprints and smudges, but inside a refrigerator or dishwasher it's the most practical finish to keep clean. All it needs is an occasional sponging with water and a nonabrasive cleanser. And if you hate scrubbing an oven, it may be worth the extra amount (about $100) for one with a self-cleaning feature.

THREE: *Check the energy-guide label.* Manufacturers are required by law to label every appliance with certain energy-related information. That information must include a description of the appliance, the model number, projected energy costs to run the appliance, a range of energy costs for similar models, and a table to estimate energy costs for running the appliance based on local utility rates.

FOUR: *Check your measurements.* Don't find out after the appliance has been delivered that it's too wide for its allocated location. Always check the measurements on your plan against the manufacturer's specifications and the actual in-store model, if possible.

FIVE: *Plan for the future.* Will the refrigerator you purchase now serve you adequately for the next dozen years? Will you be cooking more or less? If you anticipate that your household will increase or decrease in size within the next few years, reevaluate the size of any appliance model you plan to purchase and upgrade or downgrade accordingly.

SIX: *Check delivery times.* It takes a lot of patience to live through a remodeling project. You'll most likely have to do without a kitchen for what will seem like an eternity during the remodeling itself. Knowing this, the last thing you want to face is a job that's complete except for an undelivered appliance. Extended delivery times often apply to European appliances, but even if everything you order is American-made, be sure to coordinate the completion of various stages of the work with the arrival of new equipment. You should do this with your general contractor, if you will be working with one.

LIGHT BY DESIGN

Y ou may remember when modern kitchen lighting consisted of a fluorescent fixture in the middle of the ceiling that made a strange humming sound and spilled an eerie bluish color around the room. The effect was about as pleasant as the taste of canned spinach. Over the past few decades, the American palate has become more sophisticated, as has technology and society's appreciation of the role of good lighting in thoughtful design. There is probably no other room in the house that serves as many different needs as today's kitchen, and one of the ways to make it even more welcoming is to wash it in comfortable, attractive light. This chapter explores the various types of lighting and how you can use each effectively to create a functional and unique lighting plan for your design.

IN THE BEGINNING, NATURAL LIGHT

No real estate agent has ever heard a homeowner complain about too much natural light. Sunlight is so cheerful, it makes people feel good. When it streams into a room, it makes everything look better, too. With today's window technology, you can bring as much sunlight into your home as you like, and at the same time depend upon enhanced glazing options and low-E glass to solve the problem of drafty, energy-inefficient windows.

Left: *This cheerful kitchen benefits from a healthy combination of natural and artificial light. To compensate for nature's dimming effect, the owners increase the use of indoor lighting during the winter.*

On the style side, windows previously associated with custom designs, such as the "architectural" styles so popular today, are now available in standard sizes. Replacing an uninspired double-hung unit with a graceful arch-top design is relatively easy and affordable. In fact, it's not difficult to change the entire architectural look of your kitchen by simply replacing the windows. Want to transform a 50-year-old space into a stylish contemporary setting? Exchange an old window with a sleek casement-style unit. Looking for a way to add vintage character? Install a new double-hung window with snap-in muntins that imitate true divided-light windows. For drama, group individual casement or awning windows in an interesting formation along one wall. Where there is no place to add a window, you might install an operable skylight, or roof window, to bring light and air into the room.

In a country kitchen, a garden window makes a great display for plants and a natural spot for growing herbs year-round. There are also "art" styles, such as stained- and leaded-glass units, that enhance decorative or architectural styles, such as Arts and Crafts.

When considering a replacement window for the kitchen, it's important to keep in mind the architectural style both of the exterior of the house and of the other windows. If you choose a look that's different, select one that's compatible, at least. Windows are placed on the exterior of a house in a pattern. If you change either the window style or pattern of placement in one room, you may inadvertently create an eyesore on the outside of your home.

Left: *True divided-light windows in this breakfast bay bring lots of early morning eastern light into the kitchen. When the weather is warm, the windows open to let in fresh air. Recessed canister lights, overhead, assist on cloudy days and at night.*

As you consider window placement in the kitchen, also take a good look at the view you will bring indoors with a new unit. Will it create a pleasant focal point or will you face the neighbor's shed? Also consider the direction the window faces in terms of the sun throughout the day. While a southern exposure offers the most sunlight, your kitchen may get too hot—especially during the summer—unless the window is covered. A northern exposure is cool and casts the quality of light that's desirable in an artist's studio but not in a breakfast nook. Windows that face west receive lots of light in the late afternoon, which may be perfect for when the kids do their homework at the table. On the other hand, if early risers need a jolt of sunshine to get them up and running, they will appreciate a window that faces east. Whatever you decide, no matter how much natural light there is in the kitchen, you will have to supplement it with artificial light.

Window Styles

Fixed

Snap-In Muntins

Casement

Awning

Double Hung

ARTIFICIAL LIGHT

Artificial lighting is the easiest way to set or change the atmosphere of an entire room. With one switch, your kitchen can go from a bright, efficient hub of activity to a softly lit setting for a quiet meal. Plus, the right light can make meal preparation and cleanup safer and more efficient. Just think how much time you might save if you could open a cabinet and spot whatever you need right away, or how quickly you could chop an onion in a bright, clear, shadowless space. In addition, performing tasks that sometimes feel like drudgery seems easier in the right light because your eyes are less susceptible to strain. The key to devising a versatile plan that can change with each activity, as well as with the time of day, begins with knowing about the different types of artificial light.

AMBIENT LIGHT

Ambient, or general, light is illumination that fills an entire room. The source is sometimes an overhead fixture, but the light itself does not appear to come from any specific direction. The most obvious example is fluorescent strips; the covering over the strips hides the source and diffuses the light.

A wall sconce is another example of ambient light. The fixture washes light up or down the wall for an overall glow. The wall reflects the light and diminishes the look of a single source. You can tell the light is coming from the sconce, but the overall glow is diffused.

The key to good ambient lighting is making it inconspicuous. It is merely the backdrop for the rest of the room, not the main feature. It always provides light but should never become obvious. Ambient lighting used during the day should blend with the natural light that enters a room. During the evening, you should be able to diminish or soften the light level so it doesn't contrast jarringly against the blackness outside.

TASK LIGHT

Task light is purely functional. It should always be included as part of the lighting plan for any room, illuminating specif-

Left: *Even a room with lots of natural light needs supplemental artificial light. Here, a combination of recessed and track-mounted fixtures provides excellent general illumination.*

ic areas for specific jobs, such as reading a recipe or rolling out dough in a baking center. It's also essential for safety in a kitchen, especially when working around a hot stove or oven or using sharp instruments. The key to good task lighting is installing it directly over or slightly to the side of each work surface. Small lights mounted to the underside of a cabinet are an excellent example of well-thought placement. If you placed the light sources directly overhead, your body would create shadows as you bend over the work surface.

Task lighting is intended for more than just the countertop. Include it in every area of the room where you work—at the cooktop, over the sink, at the desk, above the laundry and ironing center, even above the snack bar and table. Install a separate switch for task lights; don't include them on the switch that controls the general lighting for the room. With task lighting, the ideal is to be able to turn it on and off easily whenever you need it.

ACCENT LIGHT

Often the most overlooked element in any room but always the most dramatic, accent light draws attention to a particular element, such as an interesting architectural feature or decorative object. The key here is choosing what to highlight. Don't light every object at once or they'll compete with each other. Look at the best features of your kitchen—whether built-in or decorative—and decide what underpins

Below: *Recessed fixtures installed equidistant from the range offer suitable lighting for the cooking zone. The low-voltage halogen track lights at the work island provide highly focused illumination.*

Opposite: *Miniature strip lights located inside the ceiling cove create architectural drama in the kitchen.*

DECORATIVE LIGHT

While accent light draws attention to another object or surface, decorative light draws attention to itself. It can be kinetic, in the form of candles or the glow from inside a fireplace, or static, such as a fixed wall candelabra. It doesn't highlight specific areas the way accent light does, and it doesn't provide a great deal of illumination as does ambient light, but decorative light is the device most designers love to use. Its sole purpose is to grab attention: lighting for the sake of lighting. Because it commands notice, however, it can be used indirectly to distract from something else. In this sense, it can be functional, as well. You can use decorative lighting in the kitchen to draw the eye upward toward a cathedral ceiling or to distract attention from the mess at the food preparation area. For example, candlelight on the table at dinnertime will keep everyone from noticing the pots and pans piled in the sink. By capturing your eye, decorative lighting forces your focus away from everything else.

Some sources of decorative light include candles, chandeliers, neon sculptures or signs, a strip of miniature lights—any type of light that is deliberate and contrived. Include this form of lighting to strike a balance among all lighting in the room, including natural light from the sun and moon.

the overall look you want to achieve. Use accent light to add personality to the room. Light a cooking alcove or focus attention on a handsome custom range hood. Install recessed light fixtures within a ceiling cove. Show off pretty stemware inside a glass-door cabinet by mounting small lights inside the cabinet box. Highlight a pottery or basket collection on top of cabinets with small lamps that can be masked behind crown molding. Spotlight wall art.

Accent light is purely optional, but without it there is no focus, no character to the space. With it, the room becomes an exciting, theatrical, and rich environment.

THE ROLE OF BULBS

Different types of bulbs, or "lamps" as lighting professionals call them, can affect the way your kitchen looks, feels, and functions. Does this mean you can change a few lightbulbs and forget about your remodeling project? Not likely. But you can make dramatic changes in your kitchen by switching from one type of bulb to another.

Understanding the differences in lamps will help you select the right light source for every area of your kitchen. Light is like paint: You can get different effects depending on the combinations of bulbs and fixtures you use. And color is

nothing but a reflection of different wavelengths of light energy. When selecting lamps for your kitchen, always consider the relationship between color and light.

STANDARD MEASUREMENTS FOR COLOR

Scales used in universal lighting assess the color temperature that a lamp emits and how light from the lamp affects objects it lights. The term *color temperature* describes the appearance of light in terms of the warmth or coolness of its color. Fluorescent lamps, which do not emit a continuous spectrum of light, are assigned a *correlated color temperature* (CCT) value. Lamp colors, which range from red to orange to yellow to blue to blue-white, are ranked according to the Kelvin (K) temperature scale. This rating will help you select lamps that are closely matched. You will also be able to vary the coolness or warmth of lighting for specific situations. Generally, light sources below 3,000K are considered warm, while those above 4,100K are considered cool. Different brands of bulbs may vary slightly. Also, a dimmer will shift a bulb's color toward a warmer value.

Color rendition describes how a light source affects the perception of the color of an object it illuminates. The Color Rendition Index (CRI) is a way of measuring a specific lamp's ability to read true color (the color of an object in sunlight). Color-rendering capabilities of lamps are rated from 1 to 100, with true color at 100.

TYPES OF BULBS

Most homes include a combination of warm and cool tones, so selecting bulbs that provide balanced lighting close to what appears normal to the eye is usually the most attractive choice. Experiment with balancing various combinations of bulbs to create the desired effect. To help you achieve the balance you want, here is a brief description of the different types of bulbs.

Incandescent. Like sunlight, incandescent bulbs emit *continuous-spectrum light,* or light that contains every color.

Opposite: *Hanging chrome fixtures lend an old-fashioned feeling to a remodeled kitchen with Victorian charm. An under-cabinet fixture lights the countertop; small spotlights brighten the cooking alcove.*

Illumination from these bulbs, in fact, is even warmer than sunlight, making its effect very appealing. It makes skin tones look good and enhances the feeling of well-being. Also, they come in a variety of shapes, sizes, and applications. One type even features a waterproof lens cover that makes it suitable for use near a sink or above the cooktop where steam can gather. Incandescent bulbs may be clear, diffuse, tinted, or colored, and they may have a reflective coating inside. The drawback is that incandescents use a lot of electricity and produce a lot of heat. That means they'll cost a lot more energy dollars to run.

Fluorescent. These energy-efficient bulbs cast a diffuse, shadowless light that makes them great for general illumination. They are economical, but the old standard fluorescents produce an unflattering light, making everything and everyone appear bluish and bland. Newer fluorescent bulbs, called *triphosphor fluorescent lamps,* are warmer and render color that more closely resembles sunlight. Fluorescents are available both in the familiar tube versions and in newer, compact styles. Mixing these bulbs with incandescent lamps, plus adding as much natural light to the kitchen plan as possible, can make fluorescents more appealing. Be aware, though, that in some parts of the country local codes *require* installing fluorescent lights—no other types—to conform to energy conservation mandates.

Halogen. This is actually a type of incandescent lamp that produces a brighter, whiter light at a lower wattage, with greater energy efficiency. The disadvantages are a higher price tag and higher heat output that requires special shielding. However, although halogens cost more up front, they last longer than conventional incandescents. A subcategory of halogen is the low-voltage version. It produces a 50-percent brighter light than standard halogen and is even more energy efficient. Compact in size, low-voltage halogens are typically used for creative accent lighting.

Fiber Optics. One of countless innovations gradually finding its way into the home, a fiber-optic system consists of one extremely bright lamp to transport light to one or more destinations through fiber-optic conduits. Used to accent spaces, fiber-optic lighting has the advantage of not generat-

ing excessive heat. This makes it ideal as an alternative to decorative neon lights, which get very hot and consume a great deal of energy.

ASSESSING YOUR LIGHTING NEEDS

When a room isn't bright enough, most people just exchange low-watt bulbs for high-watt versions. Wattage, however, is simply a measurement of how much electricity a lamp consumes. The light output of a bulb is actually measured in *lumens.* If the bulbs you have been using aren't providing enough general light, substitute them with ones that have more lumens. The next time you shop for bulbs, read the packaging, which indicates the lumens per watt (lpw) produced by a bulb. The more lumens per watt, the more efficient the lamp. When looking for intensity produced by a lamp, refer to its *candlepower* (Cp). The more *candela* (units), the brighter the source.

But when planning a suitable light design, you must take other factors into consideration, too. Before you do anything about buying lamps and fixtures, assess how you will use the kitchen in addition to the basic functions of cooking, eating, and cleaning up. Think about how you want it to feel—perhaps cool and efficient while you work but cozy while you dine.

Assess the reflectance levels in the room—the amount of light reflected from a colored surface, such as a tiled countertop or painted wall. Light colors and shiny surfaces are reflective, dark colors and matte surfaces are absorbent. For example, white reflects 80 percent of the light in a room, while black reflects only 4 percent. When selecting materials and colors, therefore, remember that a kitchen with light walls and cabinets and high-gloss countertops

and flooring requires less light than one with dark or matte-finished surfaces and wood cabinetry.

Next in your evaluation, consider the size of the room. How high are the ceilings? Tall ceilings require brighter lights to dispel shadows. But you'll have to tone down the brightness in a room with low ceilings because light bounces off low ceilings and walls. The number of windows in the room will also affect your kitchen's lighting needs. Do the windows face the sunny south, or is the kitchen exposure directed toward the north or somewhere in between?

Opposite: *Open coiled-metal fixtures allow the intense heat some halogen lamps generate to be safely dissipated.*

Right: *Suspended downlights hang from wires that conduct electrical current to the bulbs.*

Above: *Compact fluorescent lightbulbs (CFLs), located near the sink and above the cooktop, offer great energy efficiency and render colors and textures accurately. Although they don't produce the warm glow of incandescent lamps, they are an economical choice in the kitchen where lights are kept on for long periods of time.*

Designers typically determine lighting needs by using suggested *foot-candle* (Fc) levels for different activities and areas. Foot-candles, which refer to the amount of light that falls on a surface, are used primarily for directional lamps. To determine the foot-candle power you will need to adequately light an area, divide the candlepower of the bulb you intend to use by the distance from the fixture to the surface squared ($Fc = Cp \div D^2$).

There are no perfect stock formulas. But by looking at how each of these factors affects the others, you can make educated choices when developing your lighting plan. Keeping in mind the science and technology involved in lighting will help you determine your lighting requirements for the new kitchen. Ideally, you will want to incorporate a variety of the available options for various activities in order to create the desired ambiance and decorative effects. Use the following steps to get started.

 ONE: *Examine your activities.* Make a list of everything that occurs in your kitchen on a daily basis. Besides typical kitchen duties, such as cooking meals and cleaning up, include your hobby or craft pursuits, and anything else you do—or *would like to do*—in the kitchen, such as clipping coupons, reading the paper, or sewing. Be sure to consult other family members. Undoubtedly, there will be lots of things on your list, which only makes the lighting choices more critical. If your list gets too long, group similar tasks.

TWO: *Sketch an informal plan.* Refer to your base map or start with a new drawing. (Working on a piece of tissue paper that has been taped over your base map will do fine, too.) If your remodeling project encompasses adjoining rooms or is part of an open plan, add those areas to your sketch and design one cohesive lighting plan that flows from one space to the next. Circle all activity centers on your map: cooking and cleanup zones, baking center, garden and crafts areas, and so on.

Every task and function you do will require a different light level. For example, you'll need bright, clear light near the chopping block but something less intense at the snack bar.

And don't forget to include different *types* of light as well as the ability to adjust the intensity of the level of light in your design.

You will mark each circle with a G for general or ambient light, T for task light, A for accent light, and D for decorative light. In some places, you may want to indicate more than one. For example, if you plan on using your kitchen table for small intimate dinners and paying the bills, you might indicate A, G, and T. Identify your general lighting needs first, and then add your task lighting. Mark the spots for accent and decorative lighting on your plan last.

Even though some forms of decorative light don't require installation (candles, for example), indicate them on your plan, because they will interact at times with other types of light in your kitchen.

While energy-efficient fluorescent lighting is mandated by code in some regions for kitchen remodelings, it is an excellent choice for general lighting because these lamps often remain on for hours at a time. To select fluorescent bulbs most flattering to foods, look for those with warmer tones, represented by 3,000K to 3,500K on the light index.

Now you're ready to place your general lighting. The rule for spacing general light is to create a consistent spread of light. If your light breaks into noticeable patterns, the sources are placed too far apart. Depending on your arrangement of cabinets, general lights may be most effective if installed near work areas rather than in the center of the ceiling. Two 48-inch fluorescent tubes in one fixture are sufficient for kitchens that measure up to 120 square feet. For larger kitchens, use fixtures that accommodate four 48-inch tubes.

Recessed incandescent fixtures also provide general illumination and can be dimmed; recessed down-light fluorescent fixtures placed 6 to 8 feet apart provide the best light spread. Recessed incandescent fixtures spaced the same way also provide good general illumination.

In large kitchens, you might try perimeter lighting. Plan for two-tube recessed or surface-mounted fluorescent fixtures

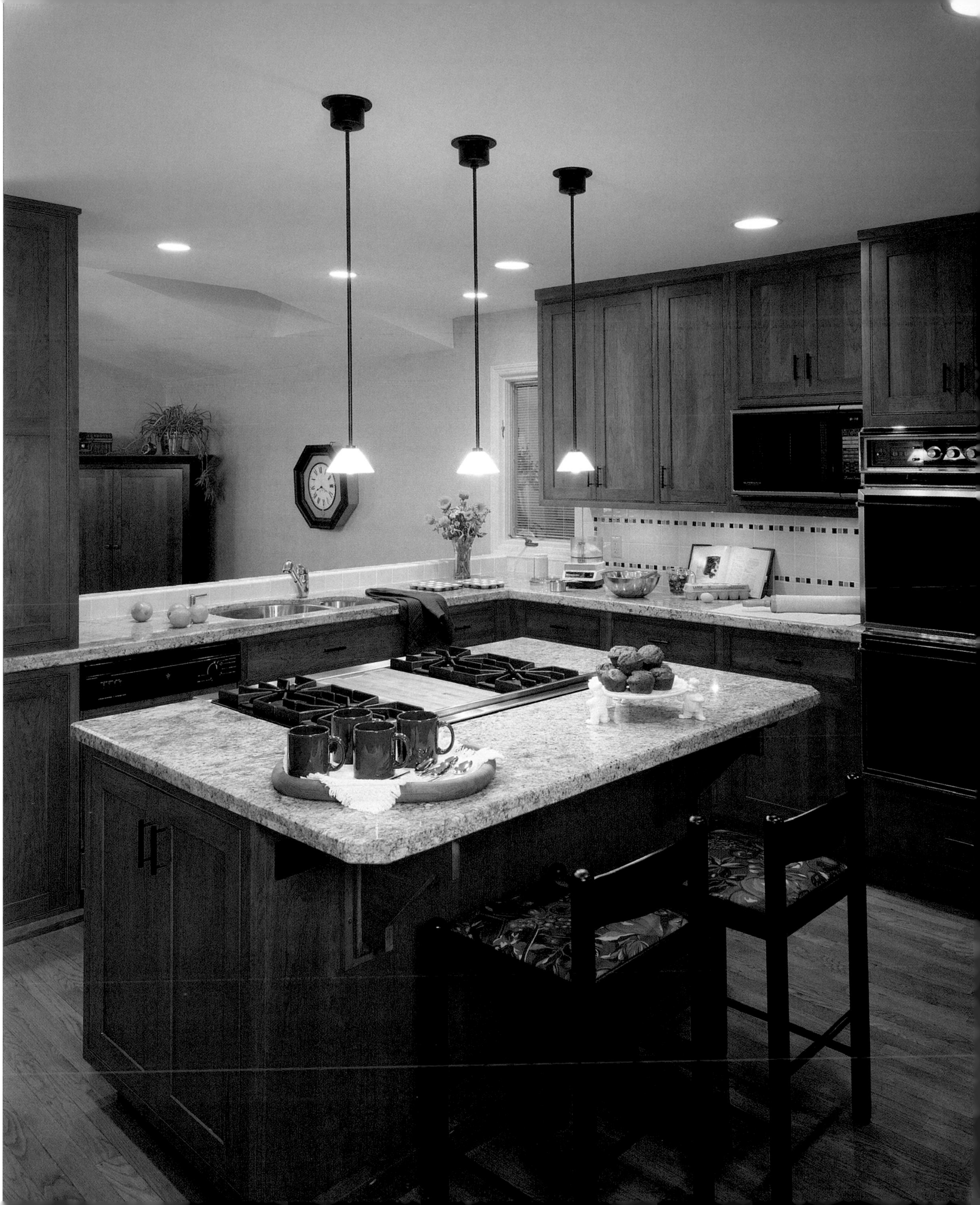

Opposite: *Decorative pendants illuminate the cooktop when meal preparation is in progress but can be dimmed for dining.*

Left: *A cooking alcove such as the one shown requires its own task lighting.*

tion is to use a thin-line fluorescent tube, which can be unobtrusively mounted behind an 8-inch face board.

Ranges. Most range hoods are equipped with fixtures that accommodate a 40- or 60-watt incandescent bulb or its equivalent, which is required for efficiency. For economy in general task lighting, substitute compact or linear fluorescent fixtures for incandescents where possible. Position any task light toward the front of the range to prevent glare, following directions given for lighting the sink area.

Countertops. Under-cabinet lighting is ideal here. Mount fixtures as close to the front of the cabinet as possible to prevent reflected glare. Choose from slim energy-efficient fluorescents, miniature track lights, or low-voltage linear systems, all of which are suitable. Use an opaque fixture or shield on the cabinet bottom to minimize glare. If you use fluorescent tubes, install one that can cover at least two-thirds of the length of the counter.

in the ceiling, over the front edge of the counter to form a square, L-, or U-shaped pattern to conform to your cabinet layout and provide general illumination. An alternative is to install recessed floodlights or fluorescent tubes in the soffit area (if there is one) above the cabinets.

Next, indicate task lighting on your plan. Your new kitchen may include special areas not related to food preparation and cleanup, but here are the typical places in every kitchen that will need illumination.

Sinks. An individual recessed down light or fixture that can be outfitted with an energy-efficient compact fluorescent lamp provides adequate task lighting when installed in the ceiling or soffit over the sink. Two incandescent down lights placed 18 inches apart on a 2-foot track or recessed and centered over the sink are also effective. Another solu-

Peninsulas and counters without upper cabinets. In a small kitchen, the general lighting fixture over the counter will have to double as a task light. If you have the space, recess or surface-mount fixtures 20 inches apart, centered over the counter. For this area, use 75-watt reflector floodlights or equivalent compact fluorescent lamps or miniature low-voltage pendants.

Islands or booths. One or more decorative pendants are suitable for use. Installed with dimmers, these lights

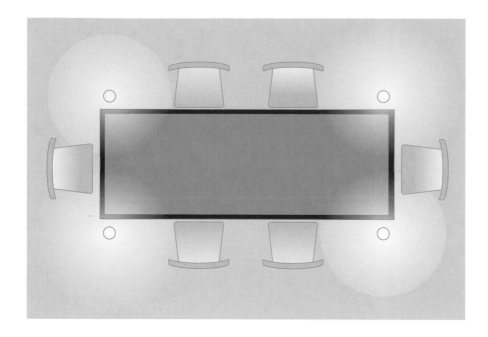

If your kitchen table has a glass top, your fixture's reflection may produce unpleasant glare. Augment or replace chandelier lighting with track or recessed fixtures. Use a ring of four down lights around the table's edge or on each side of the centered chandelier over a long table. Smaller recessed housings are effective, and low-voltage recessed lighting can create an appealing ambiance especially when used with a dimmer.

THREE: *Check your local code.* Every municipality has strict regulations regarding the type of fixtures you can use and the placement of light and electricity around water. If you want to pass inspection, be sure you don't violate codes by specifying a lamp that isn't allowed in your area or by installing a fixture too close to an area that's exposed to water.

FOUR: *Visit lighting showrooms.* The best way to learn about your options is to visit lighting showrooms. You can often take advantage of free in-store consultations. If your plan is complicated or if you have questions that require at-home consultation, you may be pleasantly surprised at the modest fee charged by a lighting specialist.

FINDING THE RIGHT FIXTURE

There is practically an endless number of lighting-fixture styles designed to match any décor and catch everyone's imagination. The past few years have proved to be a lighting designer's dream, as fixtures have become more decorative and lighting schemes more varied and eclectic. From nostalgic reproductions to architecture-inspired designs and contemporary styles, fixtures suit any look, and take the form of wall sconces, chandeliers, recessed canister lights, track lights, ceiling fixtures, and novelty types—and they come in every finish imaginable.

The copious selection of finishes offers lots of excitement, too. Look for everything from enamels to brass, chrome,

provide atmosphere perfect for dining. Figure on a total of about 120 watts incandescent or 32 to 40 watts fluorescent to light a booth. Miniature, low-voltage pendants equipped with tiny halogen bulbs add a contemporary look.

❦ **Lighting over the table.** In a kitchen with a conventional 8-foot-high ceiling, install a fixture so that its bottom is 27 to 36 inches above the table. Raise it 3 inches for every additional foot of ceiling height. With a chandelier, consider the height of the backs of the dining chairs when deciding how high to place it. Place the fixture higher for tall ladderback chairs; install it lower for short captain's chairs. Chandeliers or pendants with down lights bring out the sparkle in tableware, especially crystal. Bulbs totaling 200 to 300 watts are sufficient to light most tables, but a minimum of 150 watts is needed. For up lighting, experiment with decorative bulbs; clear or frosted bulbs are handsome with materials such as wood or wrought iron, while incandescent or amber bulbs in traditional fixtures give the impression of candlelight.

With a pendant, such as Tiffany-style lamp, there should be an open top to provide upward light. Underneath, a diffusing bowl, disk, or semi-opaque bulb will help eliminate any glare. Make sure the bulb does not extend below the edge of the shade.

pewter, nickel, and copper, which can be brushed, matted, or antiqued. There are also vintage designs in wrought iron and verdigris. For added interest, select fixtures with a combination of finishes, such as verdigris with antique brass or copper paired with wrought iron. Whatever you choose, stick to a style that is compatible with other decorative elements in the room.

Anywhere family meals are eaten deserves good, convivial lighting. In addition, providing adequate task lighting, especially in the cooking area, where sharp knives, scalding and burning materials, and the subtleties of fine cooking coexist, only makes good sense. The placement of fixtures may vary depending on the size of your kitchen. But above all, let your lighting needs dictate how many fixtures to buy and where to install them.

Opposite: *This drawing illustrates the proper placement of recessed fixtures, which we located just off the four table corners for a subtle effect.*

Below: *You'll have to judge how high or low to hang a chandelier over a table by the height of the chair backs.*

ADDING PERSONALITY TO YOUR KITCHEN

Giving your new kitchen personality requires the same careful thought dedicated to decorating any other room in the house. In fact, in homes where families spend a great deal of time in their kitchens, the motivation to make the space as comfortable and attractive as possible is even stronger. State-of-the-art equipment certainly makes life easier, but who wants a kitchen that resembles the space shuttle?

If you already have ideas about how you want your kitchen to look, you're off to a great start. But if you're still weighing the warmth and casual feeling of country décor against the grace and formality of a traditional setting, examine some of the elements that make up different decorating styles. Look at art books, and pay close attention to furniture styles, which are influencing today's cabinet design. Think about favorite decorating themes from other rooms in the house that can be carried into the kitchen using color, pattern, and finishing materials to unify your home's overall décor. In this chapter you'll get some ideas about identifying what look is right for you and how to pull all the elements together seamlessly into one coordinated decorating scheme.

Left: *An eclectic, whimsical mixture of vibrant colors and unique accessories puts a personal spin on a professional designer's own kitchen.*

DEFINING YOUR STYLE

The first rule of decorating is simple: Please yourself. While you may want to emulate a certain style or capture the feeling of a photo clipped from a magazine, don't become a slave to it and squash your creative spirit along the way. The key is to build a room around a theme while carefully incorporating your personality. A favorite color is one good way to do this, or a repeated motif.

When considering style, everyone needs inspiration. Forget the latest trends; consider rooms you have admired and the features that attracted you. Was it a painted finish on the cabinetry? The color or pattern of the wallpaper or window treatment? A handsome wood floor? A pretty collection displayed in a hutch or on a wall? How did the room make you feel? Cheerful? Relaxed? Animated? Nostalgic? This is the kind of thinking that eventually results in a finished design you will never tire of and will continue to enjoy year after year.

In addition, look for clues in the rest your house. Study its architecture. Is it contemporary? Colonial? Victorian? An Arts and Crafts-style bungalow? Is there elaborate trimwork, or are the walls, doors, and windows streamlined and spare? Even if the architecture is nondescript, you can introduce a period flavor in the room with reproduction cabinets and fixtures, window treatments, wallpaper, and accessories. Is there a theme you have already established with furnishings and decoration? Do you like antiques

or modern art? Are you a collector or someone who prefers pared-down space? You can build on these features and preferences or depart from them entirely. Just find one transitional element, such as the floor treatment or color scheme, to create a visual bridge so the change from room to room isn't too abrupt. If your kitchen will open onto other areas, such as the family room, link the two spaces with related materials; for example, coordinate the fabric used for the family room's window treatment with the kitchen wallpaper.

Whatever you do, your approach to decorating the new kitchen should be deliberate. Let it evolve over time; don't rush your choices. Live with paint, tile, and wallpaper samples for a while. This chapter offers a brief description of popular decorating styles. Feel free to follow them or design a variation on one of these themes. The colors, patterns, and other materials offered are just suggestions. Refer to them as starting points, but let your own preferences be your guide in the end. If you're not sure about something, don't do it.

Above: *Refurbished chrome and vinyl-upholstered stools outfit a small snack bar that fits neatly around a tiny corner of the room.*

Opposite: *The designer/homeowner refinished this built-in cabinet with water-based blackboard paint, which creates an erasable surface for scribbling or writing messages.*

Smart Tip about Mixing Styles

An eclectic look is sophisticated but hard to pull off. Unless you are experienced in design and feel very confident about your choices, you may want to stick with one style. However, if you do want to try mixing them, keep in mind that some styles work well together while others do not. One look that never fails to appear dramatic is the pairing of traditional architecture with ultra-modern furnishings.

Find common elements in different styles that will make them work together. Good examples of compatible looks include country and traditional or Shaker. In a contemporary setting, you can incorporate a few elements of *one* of these: Art Deco, Arts and Crafts, or Shaker style.

TRADITIONAL STYLE

Today's traditional style incorporates elements of English and American eighteenth- and early nineteenth-century design. Marked by symmetry and balance and enhanced by the look of fine-crafted details, it is dignified, rich, and formal.

Choose wood cabinetry finished with a cherry or mahogany stain or painted white, with details like fluted panels, beaded trim, bull's-eye corner blocks, and dentil and crown molding. For the door style, a raised cathedral panel (top slightly arched) is typical. An elegant countertop fabricated from marble or a plastic laminate faux version fits well into this setting, as do hand-painted tiles. Polished brass hardware and fittings will add an Old World touch.

Colors to consider include classic Wedgwood blue or deep jewel tones. Windows and French doors with true divided lights or double-hung units with pop-in muntins have great traditional-style appeal. Dress them with formal curtain panels or swags. Botanical-inspired patterns, as well as formal stripes and tapestry or crewelwork look-alikes, can tie the room's elements together.

Furnish this kitchen with an antique or reproduction hutch, where you can display formal china, and a table and chairs in traditional Windsor or Queen Anne style.

Traditional-Style Smart Tip You don't have to replace your kitchen cabinetry to get some of the fine furniture-quality details discussed above. Prefabricated trims may be purchased at local lumber mills and home centers. For example, crown molding, applied to the top of existing cabinetry and stained or painted to match the door style, may be all you need. Likewise, you can replace old hardware with reproduction polished-brass door and drawer knobs or pulls for a finishing touch.

Right: *Simple elegance defines this traditional-style kitchen. A graceful arched window, reminiscent of Palladian architecture, provides a focal point over the sink. To capture more sunlight, the designer created a backsplash of muntin-glass windows. The two central islands—one for cooking, the other for the serving—feature black-granite countertops that appear appropriately formal in this setting.*

CONTEMPORARY STYLE

What's referred to as "contemporary" style evokes images of clean architectural lines; an absence of decoration and color; and materials like chrome, glass, and stone. Indeed, its roots are at the turn of the last century, when architects and designers flatly rejected the exaggerated artificial embellishments of the Victorians by turning to natural products and pared-down forms. Various modern movements, evolving over the course of the industrialized twentieth century, gradually incorporated new man-made materials into their streamlined forms. Hence the high-tech look popularized in the 1970s and 1980s.

Today, contemporary style is taking a softer turn, even in the kitchen, a place where hard edges, cool reflective surfaces, and cutting-edge technology abound. Kitchen designers are taking another look at time-honored forms and giving them a new spin. It's not unusual to see updated versions of traditional fixtures and fittings or new uses for natural materials in a contemporary kitchen, especially as improved finishes make these products more durable and easier to maintain. And although black and white are classic mainstays in a contemporary room, the stark white palette of the last two decades has been replaced with earthy hues or warmer shades of white.

Opposite: *Old wooden chairs and a stone tabletop are two natural materials that complement one another in the kitchen.*

Left: *In this new contemporary-style kitchen, the warmth of wood cabinets, frameless and sleek, counterbalances cool materials like stainless steel, chrome, and glass.*

outdoors into this room as possible. Install casement-style windows, skylights, or roof windows to blend with contemporary architecture. Easy access to adjoining outdoor living spaces, such as decks or open-air kitchens, is highly desirable. For window treatments, Roman shades or vertical blinds offer a crisp, tailored look.

Stay with metals for lighting fixtures and hardware. Chrome, pewter, or nickel would work well. Keep your eye on function, not frills. The contemporary room revels in the pure architecture of the space.

Furnishings for a contemporary kitchen tend to have a sleek architectural look, too. In fact, much of what is considered classic contemporary furniture has been designed by well-known twentieth-century architects. Chair and table legs are typically straight, with no turnings or ornamentation. For a sophisticated look, mix complementary materials; for example, pair a glass table with upholstered chairs or a metal table with wood chairs. Display contemporary pottery on a shelf or inside a glass cabinet.

Contemporary-Style Smart Tip Incorporate elements of Arts and Crafts, Art Deco, or other designs associated with the modern movements of the twentieth century; their clean, geometric lines are quite compatible with this environment. This eclectic approach can result in a sophisticated look. Shop for framed fine art prints, vintage-inspired wallpaper, or reproduction hardware, faucets, or light fixtures to underscore your theme.

When selecting cabinets for your contemporary kitchen, pair a frameless door with a wood finish. Laminate cabinetry is still compatible with this style, but for an updated look, wood is it. Although a contemporary room is often monochromatic or neutral, don't be afraid to use color or to mix several materials or finishes, such as wood and metal. Combinations of wood and various metals—stainless steel, chrome, copper, brass, and pewter on surfaces like cabinet doors, countertops, and floors—make strong statements, as do stone and glass. Creative combinations like these keep the overall appearance of the room sleek but not sterile. For more visual interest, apply a glazed or textured finish to neutral-colored walls. And bring as much of the

Opposite: *Wood cabinets, painted apple green and trimmed with antique glass knobs, butcher-block countertops, and gingham fabric, offset the high-tech look of modern appliances.*

Left: *It's typical in a country kitchen to make an open display of utilitarian objects alongside decorative ones. In this case, the white pottery is as appealing as the cutting boards and old rolling pins.*

place will definitely add charm to your country kitchen, too, but a simple potted herb garden on the windowsill will do so, too.

Wood floors are a natural choice in this setting, although terra cotta tiles are an attractive accent to a European-inspired country setting. Be sure to add throw rugs, preferably braided or woven rag, in front of the sink and range for added comfort underfoot.

For a custom touch, add a stenciled backsplash or wall border. If you want a truly individual look, try a faux finish like sponging, ragging, combing, or rubbed-back plaster. These techniques are fun, and easy and add texture to your walls, providing a richer, warmer feeling. For a Continental flavor, apply a glaze that imitates a rustic fresco finish. Use the space in the soffit area or above a window to hang herbs for drying.

Install double-hung windows. (Standard casement windows look too contemporary in this setting.) Finish them with full trim, and top them with simple cotton curtains, or just install valances. Don't overdress them.

Country-Style Smart Tip Keep it simple, and avoid cutesy clutter. A *touch* of whimsy is fine and always looks at home in a country kitchen, especially when it is handcrafted. One way to achieve a country look is with hardware. Pick up an accent color from the tile or wallpaper, and paint unfinished knobs and pulls, which are available at craft stores. Or mix and match standard metal or glass pieces with a few fun ones. Designs you might consider include fruit, vegetable, or animal motifs.

COUNTRY STYLE

Whether you call it American, French, English, Italian, or Scandinavian, this style is always a favorite because of its basic, casual, relaxed feeling. In fact, every country has its own version. "Country" implies a deeper connection to the outdoors and the simple life than other styles and uses an abundance of natural elements. Start off with plain wood cabinetry stained a light maple, or add a distressed, crackled, or pickled finish. This is the perfect kitchen for mixing different finishes because unmatched pieces underpin the informal ambiance of a country room. Cabinet door styles are typically framed, sometimes with a raised panel. Beadboard cabinets are a typical American country choice. Or leave the doors off, allowing colorful dishes and canned and boxed goods to create a fun display. For the countertop, install butcher block or hand-painted or silk-screened tiles. Another option is a colorful or patterned countertop fabricated from inlaid solid-surfacing material. A working fire-

THE COTTAGE LOOK

This vintage look, inspired by quaint English-country style, is appealing in the kitchen because it's cozy, casual, and warm. Framed wood cabinets with an unfitted or unmatched appearance—especially in a mix of finishes, such as a honey maple paired with a color stain that looks aged or distressed—provide a good starting point for building on this theme. Muntin-glass doors and built-in open plate or pot racks and display shelves should be part of the cabinetry's design. Milk- or clear-glass knobs and pulls will dress the cabinets nicely, or use forged metal hardware for a rustic appearance.

Beadboard on the walls or ceiling always looks at home in this style kitchen, as does brick. Use brick as a backsplash or as a surround at the cooker. An English import, the AGA cooker, is a great way to bring the old-time European look of a cast-iron stove into the room while providing all the modern-day conveniences. (See Chapter Six, "Major Appliances & More.") Install an exposed-apron (farmhouse-style) sink with a reproduction chrome and porcelain faucet set to add more charm. On the floor, use wide wood planks or stone with a colorful hand-painted floorcloth on top. Something with a pattern of big, chubby blooms would be attractive. Bring more color into the room with blue-green surfaces accented in varying shades of rose and cream.

A double-hung window lends a traditional note, but if you can make the style work with the exterior of your house, a Gothic-inspired architectural design would tie it all together. This style, with Medieval roots, was popular with the Victorians. Accent with lighting fixtures that resemble old-fashioned gas lamps.

For furniture, include a good-size farmhouse table in your plan, as well as a Welsh dresser and plate rack for displaying a pretty collection of Majolica or similar earthenware.

The Cottage-Look Smart Tip For authenticity, the overall look has to appear slightly worn, but not shabby. You can accomplish this by distressing wood surfaces, such as a tabletop, or adding a crackle finish to woodwork. Another idea is to use a natural dye on table linens or cotton fabric window treatments. Compared with synthetics, these dyes seem slightly faded and will lend a comfortable lived-in feeling to your cottage-style kitchen.

Below, left: *An old dresser and hutch and faded, vintage linens bring their own brand of cottage charm to this kitchen.*

Below, right: *The stone tile floor, the wall-mounted rack for herb drying, an old armoire, and the unfitted look of the cabinetry combine to create this cozy informal look.*

Opposite: *Rustic pine cabinets, yellow walls, tiles, and the collection of blue and white plates and platters displayed on the walls suggest a French-country farmhouse as inspiration for this kitchen. An old wooden table and an antique wrought-iron chandelier are excellent furniture choices to carry out the theme.*

PROVENÇAL STYLE

This French-country style evokes images of the Mediterranean and warm, sunny days. Its origins go back to the one- and two-room farmhouses of southern France built centuries ago, when the kitchen was a large communal room. To recreate its charming ambiance, whitewash walls or apply a subtle glaze finish in an earth tone, such as rose ocher or sienna. Install wood on the ceiling beams with an aged or distressed look.

Original Provençal kitchens had large limestone hearths and, of course, working fireplaces. Your modern-day version may or may not have a working fireplace, but you can introduce limestone by installing it on the floor. Otherwise, use rustic clay tiles, which also have a warm, earthy appeal. For the appearance of a hearth, design a cooking alcove to house the range or cooktop. Accent it with colorful tiles or brick. Create a focal point at the cooking area with a handsome copper range hood. Hang a rack for copper pots and sauce pans. Carry the copper over to the sink; one with a hammered finish will look spectacular. Since it will need a little extra care, you may want to reserve the copper for the bar sink and use a more practical porcelain model—preferably a deep one with an exposed apron—for heavy-duty use. Pair that sink with a simple wall-mounted chrome faucet that has a high-arc spout.

Unfitted cabinetry in the form of a dresser with shelves, a cupboard, or an armoire is quintessential to this style, but you'll probably need storage that is more practical and efficient for contemporary use, too. One way to achieve this is to substitute wall cabinets for open shelves, then use one of the pieces of furniture as an accent and for extra storage. Include wrought-iron hardware in your design, which will coordinate with a wrought iron chandelier or baker's rack.

Decorate with provincial mini-print fabrics and wallcoverings in mustard yellow, clay red, and the deep blue that is inspired by the lavender that grows all over the region. For authenticity, paint window and door trims blue. Dress windows with lace café curtains and stencil a pretty *fleur de lis* border around the trim.

Add details, such as flavored oils and vinegars displayed in pretty glass bottles, fresh herbs growing from racks in sunny windows, and blue and white tiles.

Provençal-Style Smart Tip No country kitchen would be complete without a massive harvest table. If you can't find an affordable antique, create your own. Buy a long, unfinished pine table, and stain it a rich walnut color. Because pine is a soft wood, you won't have to add "authentic" distress marks because normal wear and tear will do that for you. Pair the table with an assortment of unmatched chairs to add casual ambiance.

SHAKER STYLE

The basic tenets of the Shaker philosophy, which evolved out of a nineteenth-century religious movement, are built on a sense of humility. "Beauty rests on utility," was their belief. This was reflected in their homes. They believed in using only the most essential elements, completely without ornamentation or frills. Their plain, practical designs featured dovetailed joints and hand-planed tops, plain panels on doors, and legs tapered almost to a pencil point. The finishes on original Shaker cabinets were always dyes and oils, never varnishes, to enhance the wood.

Contemporary cabinet manufacturers, responding to a renewed popularity of the Shaker look during the last decade, have used the Shakers' original designs to inspire similar updated versions of their own. When shopping for Shaker-style cabinetry, look for the same plain paneled doors and wood finishes that are finished to hold up against moisture and grease today. When stained to match the cabinets, a typical Shaker rack of slanted shelves, whether left freestanding or mounted to the wall, makes a great accent piece. Stack a few round, wooden Shaker boxes on the shelves; you can find them, unfinished, in craft stores. Paint them with a color picked up from the woodwork or something else in the kitchen.

Keeping simplicity in mind, paint the walls in a Shaker-inspired kitchen white. Accent woodwork in colors inspired by natural dyes—terra cotta, yellow ochre, olive green, green-blue, and denim. Ceramic tile installed in a quiltlike pattern on the countertop or backsplash, or as a mural above the cooktop or on the range hood can add more color accents and a reasonable amount of decoration, unless you're a purist at heart. The fixtures should be white or crème-tone with plain fittings in a brushed chrome or pewter finish. Trim kits, available from appliance and cabinet manufacturers, can camouflage modern-day appliances so they blend; Shakers eschewed such modern conveniences.

A traditional double-hung window, with or without muntins, fits in fine with the Shaker theme. Install plain wood shutters and panel-style curtains with tab tops fabricated in simple cotton. A tin chandelier paired with tin wall sconces will pull the look together.

Shaker-inspired furniture is widely available today. Tall ladder-back chairs with tape-woven seats look at home around a simple trestle table. A pegged chair rail is a Shaker classic. Installed high on the wall, it can be a display for a collection of handwoven baskets, dried flowers, tapered candles, or even small wooden chairs.

Shaker-Style Smart Tip This warm, likable style fits perfectly with a country home because of its old-fashioned look. But it blends well with contemporary interiors, too, because of its clean lines and plain geometric shapes. In fact, a few Shaker elements can warm up the sometimes cold appearance of a contemporary room.

Left: *The cotton-tape chair backs and seats are inspired by traditional Shaker designs. The distinctive pommels on top were used originally to grasp the chair and carry it to a peg rail.*

Opposite: *Shakers often left their kitchen windows unadorned because they loved natural light.*

CUCINA RUSTICA

ARTS and CRAFTS STYLE

The Arts and Crafts movement, with roots at the turn of the twentieth century, was a reaction to the ornamentation of Victorian design and the growing use of machines to produce cheap goods. It also professed a philosophy that beautiful, simple, organic objects arranged harmoniously in a house will contribute to one's well-being. The movement's aesthetic is enjoying a resurgence today. Styles that are related to or part of the Arts and Crafts movement include Mission, Craftsman, and Prairie, the signature style of the architect Frank Lloyd Wright.

Start with plain oak cabinets with a handcrafted appearance. As with Shaker style, manufacturers are responding to the public interest in Arts and Crafts, and some offer a line of authentically inspired cabinets. Accessorize with hand-hammered copper hardware. If you can't find genuine examples, shop for reproductions.

The more wood the better in an Arts and Crafts-style room. Oil the wood well to bring out the grain, and properly seal it against water damage.

For the walls, combine oak wainscoting with a stylized wallpaper—one that combines floral motifs with a geometric pattern; there are wallpaper manufacturers that specialize in this. Select colors that reflect natural hues, such as brown, green, blue, and orange. Accessorize with organically shaped pottery in these colors, too. Pull it all together by incorporating Native American textiles, such as a rug, into this room.

You might want to design a custom-tiled backsplash with matte or "art pottery" glazed tiles. Your lighting design can include a combination of fixtures, such as unobtrusive recessed ceiling canisters and wall lamps with Tiffany-style glass covers or mica shades.

Opposite: *Natural materials take center stage in this setting. The generous use of windows makes the landscape a part of the interior design of the kitchen.*

Right: *These new glass shades are faithful reproductions of Arts and Crafts style.*

Plain windows should be curtained very simply—if at all—in an Arts and Crafts-style room, using natural fabrics such as linen or muslin with an embroidered border. Typical motifs include ginkgo leaves and poppy seeds. Instead of traditional treatments, use stained glass or art-glass windows: Several manufacturers produce an Arts and Crafts line of stained-glass types. To complete the look, furnish the kitchen with a Mission-style table and chairs and a hutch, if there is room for one.

Arts and Crafts-Style Smart Tip The heart of this style lies in its earthy connection. The more you can bring nature into it, the more authentic it will appear. An easy way to do this is with plants. Open the space up to nature with glass doors that provide a view to a green garden.

THE DECORATING PHASE

Once you've determined the style that suits your personality, you can begin to take the steps that will pull the entire project together. Remember, using a particular style as a guideline is helpful, but listen to your own instincts. Begin this creative phase in your kitchen project by following these simple steps:

SMART STEPS

ONE: *Create a sample board.* Don't make your kitchen decorating all trial and error. Try your ideas out on a sample board first. To make one, use a piece of 1/2-inch plywood, which is heavy enough to hold your samples but light enough for you to handle. Mount your samples—paint chips, wallpaper swatches, flooring and tile samples, countertop chips, and any other materials you plan to bring into the room—on the board to see how each works as part of the overall scheme. The larger the sample, the better. If a wallpaper pattern clashes with the color or pattern of the tile, change one or both until you find a match that works. The board lets you test your ideas before you start buying materials and risk costly mistakes.

Try different combinations, and look at them in all light levels, night and day. Add photographs of fixtures, appliances, cabinetry, and other items you will include in the room for which you don't have samples to put on the board.

Create a "cheat sheet" to take with you when you shop. (Your full-size sample board is a wonderful resource for building a room that works in harmony, but it will be too awkward to carry with you.) Remembering color shades accurately is nearly impossible. Working without a guide is a sure way to end up with something that doesn't match.

When creating your sample board, include your sources. Note store names for every item, as well as manufacturers and prices. If there are model numbers and color names, note them too. This will be invaluable if you ever have to touch up or replace an item later. A smart trick to remembering wallpaper or paint-shade names is to write them on the back of outlet plates during the remodeling.

After completing your project, keep the sample board; it may come in handy if you decide to redecorate the adjoining rooms. With all your samples, it won't be difficult to achieve a cohesive or compatible style.

TWO: *Note the sight lines.* A sight line is the visual path the eye follows from a given point within a room or from an entrance. A room's primary sight line is the entry. It's the most important one because it draws your attention into

the room. Your eye immediately moves in one direction toward whatever is directly opposite the doorway. It may be the range or the door to a backyard garden, but very often in a kitchen it will be the window over the sink. Hopefully, the view is a pleasant one that makes an excellent case for enlarging the window. If possible, install one in a dramatic architectural style. However, if the view is not desirable, an attractive window treatment that is easy to adjust

when you want to let in light or close out the outdoors is a good idea. Also, an appealing arrangement of healthy potted plants can help disguise a less-than-perfect view.

If the kitchen entry is located in the middle of the space, the sight line could be a monotonous bank of solid cabinetry, or worse: the dishwasher. Hopefully, this is not the case. The time for relocating major appliances and cabinets is not at the decorating stage; however, if you're still in the planning process and reading this chapter for ideas, review your base map and Chapter Two, "Creating Functional Space," to see whether you can rearrange things. Remember: A kitchen normally has two or three dominant sight lines governing it's design, and you have to consider the sight lines going into the room as well as those going from it.

Left: *The sight line from the kitchen into the adjoining dining/family room is an attractive view to the outdoors.*

Above: *The blue tile on the backsplashes and countertops, as well as the use of the same floor tile, carry the eye from one separate area to the next.*

Inside the kitchen, you may want to situate your table and chairs or snack counter so that when people are seated they don't have to look at the food-preparation area or stare at a wall. Again, if at all possible a view to the outdoors is ideal, but even looking at an attractive collection of pottery artfully arranged in a hutch or a *trompe l'oeil* window painted on a wall is preferable to facing dirty pots and pans.

Move to other places where you are apt to linger and examine the sight lines. If you entertain in the kitchen, where do guests congregate? At the counter where you set up the buffet? Around the table? If the kitchen is open to other areas of the house, such as the family room, step into those areas and note what you can see when you look into the kitchen. Maybe all you'll have to do is resituate the dining table.

Don't just think about what you don't want to see. Use sight lines to focus attention on attractive elements and to move your eye around the space. Sight lines should be fluid; you don't want the eye to jump from one element to the next. Visual appreciation should flow. The angle of the range hood should draw the eye to the cooktop, for example. The faucet should pull the eye to the sink, then down the counter. The island should make the eye want to travel the length and depth of it before canvassing the outer edges of the room.

Plan your kitchen's sight lines with balance and symmetry in mind. Don't place all of the most powerful visual elements on one side of the room. Find ways to attract attention to all four walls. There should be something interesting to see in all directions but not so much that everything clashes.

THREE: *Add details.* More than anything else, people react to and remember a room's details—the special touches that take style one step further to a personal level. Details have a powerful effect on the feeling and mood of a room. They usually make the difference between a space that looks professionally designed and one that lacks polish.

Some of the best details are the smallest—exquisite hardware, handsome molding, a stenciled soffit, or a tiled mural, to name a few. Or they could be accessories such as a collection of salt and pepper shakers, antique tins, molds, or other kitchenware, or framed prints grouped on a wall.

When creating an arrangement of objects, keep scale and proportion in mind. A large object on a small surface looks awkward, a small object on a large surface appears lost. When grouping three or more things, balance one large object with several smaller ones. Keep wall displays at eye level—whether you are standing or sitting. You'll have to adjust them so that they are at a comfortable height in either position. If a grouping is on the wall behind the table, don't hang it where it can be bumped by someone's head when seated. First, sketch the arrangement to scale on paper, especially if you plan to hang it on the wall. Don't be afraid to group dissimilar objects. Link them by theme or color. For example, use the same color mat board to coordinate a collection of unrelated framed items. Or paint the frames the same hue.

FOUR: *Use color.* Color is probably your greatest decorating tool. Don't be afraid of it—it's also one of the easiest things to change. You may want to stick with white or another neutral for permanent fixtures and equipment, although it's possible to change the color of appliances using automotive paint. (Check the Yellow Pages or call an automotive shop to inquire about this service.) But you could opt for color on your cabinets—even as a detail on the molding or on just one section. (See Chapter Five, "Cabinetry & Storage.") If the cabinets are wood, you can repaint them later if you want to do something different to the room or change the color.

If you are more daring, you could introduce color with your countertop or flooring. Neither of these is necessarily easy or inexpensive to replace if you tire of it, but they aren't major projects, either, especially if they are standard installations of moderately priced materials. However, avoid trendy colors that will date your kitchen; leave most of the color to your walls and accessories.

One of the best ways to test a color is to apply it to a sheet of white poster board, hang it on the wall, and live with it for a few days. Look at it during the day; then wait for

Left: *Color and the way it is applied can make any place special. In this kitchen's small dining area, big, bold, squares, handpainted in citrus green and white, make the space appear larger.*

evening and look at it again under varying light levels. Does it still appeal to you? What effect does it have on the space at different times of the day? Does it make it appear larger or smaller, warmer or cooler? Do this test for paint, wallpaper, window treatments, tile, and flooring. For an item with a print, find a paint that matches the dominant color, and apply the same test to it.

Color has amazing properties. It can evoke memories, create a mood, or even change your perception of space. Light colors expand a room; dark ones draw the walls in. This is also true of ceilings. If you have a high ceiling that makes your kitchen feel more like a barn, paint the ceiling a deeper shade than the walls to tone down the volume of the space and make the room feel cozier. Visually you are creat-

ing an optical illusion that will affect your emotional response to the space, as well.

As a rule of thumb, use no more than three colors in a room. For interest, apply them in varying amounts, shades, and tints. You might want to avoid a monochromatic scheme, however, because it tends to become boring. If you are completely set on using one color only, liven it up by adding shading, pattern, and texture. Try a painted finish like ragging, sponging, or glazing.

The stronger the color, the less of it should be used. That's another general rule, which can be broken by personal preference. Remember: A dollop of saturated red equals an entire wall of pale pink in visual interpretation.

When you use two or three colors, combine unequal amounts and different shades of each, along with a dash of black, white, or another neutral. If you don't do this, your eyes won't know where to focus. Let one color dominate. Anchor accent colors in opposite parts of the room. For example, you can pick up one color from the wallpaper in the curtains, then use the same color for the cushions on chairs or stools.

Where do you get your color inspiration? For an explosion of color, visit the produce aisle of a grocery store or the local garden nursery. Comb through fashion magazines and art books. Look inside your clothes closet. Tear out pictures of anything with color that attracts you. Keep a record in your design notebook. After you've got a stack of tearsheets, separate them by color. Undoubtedly a pattern will emerge. Whatever color dominates that collection is a good indicator of what pleases you most of the time.

WALLPAPER, PAINT, AND FABRIC IN THE KITCHEN

While you're thinking about color for the kitchen, consider the type of paint, wallpaper, and fabric to use. Anything that isn't washable should be out of the question. Dust and grime cling to the grease that accumulates in a kitchen—no matter how much venting you install and how meticulous you are about wiping up spills and spatters. And germs thrive around moisture—not just at the sink but at the cooktop, too. Just look at the wet wall behind your range the next time you steam vegetables.

Luckily, it isn't difficult to find materials and products that are designed to hold up better and clean more easily than ever before. Some paints, wallpapers, wallpaper glues, and fabrics also contain a mildewcide, which may be an advantage if your kitchen doesn't get enough ventilation.

After you've chosen a color scheme, look for wallpaper and fabrics to carry your theme through. You can also use wallpaper to suggest a theme or decorative style in the kitchen. Many manufacturers have produced new designs that reinterpret historical motifs, for example. Use them, later, to pick up a solid color for accents or trim. However, two major factors influencing what patterns to choose are the location and the size of the kitchen.

Before doing anything,, review the sight lines from outside the room and any adjoining spaces, especially any areas you must pass through to get to the kitchen. Think of them sequentially. Ideally, there should be an interrelationship among all the patterns and colors that run from room to room. If you want stripes in the kitchen but an adjoining area has a floral print, match the colors.

In a small kitchen, as a rule, a bold print may be too busy. On the other hand, it may be just what's needed to make a large space cozier. Vertical designs will make the ceiling appear higher and tailored; horizontal patterns will move your eye from one corner to the next; random patterns will add an informal feeling. In general, traditional-style rooms look best with patterned wallpaper. In contemporary settings, subtle patterns that don't detract from the architectural lines of a room are best. And always avoid trendy motifs unless you want to make changes every couple of years.

Opposite: *The homeowner used just enough of this yellow-green paint shade to freshen the older kitchen's appearance. Other surfaces are kept white to temper this citus-like hue.*

Below: *In this kitchen, red walls warm up the room, make it cozier, and counterbalance the cool whiteness of the finish on the cabinets and appliances.*

REMODELING TIMELINE AT A GLANCE

There are many variables that can affect the pace and timing of your kitchen remodeling project. Every contractor works differently, and each job may present its own small—or large—glitches. However, there are steps that divide up the process into logical sequences that eventually result in a finished design.

Here's a timeline of events that will help you gauge the work that is involved, in a sequential fashion. The time lengths indicated for the various stages are for an average-size kitchen project using standard products and materials. Keep in mind that the time indicated is approximate. Depending on the scope of your kitchen remodeling, it may be shorter or longer. If you order custom cabinets or imported materials, they will require an 8- to 12-week lead time that will hold up the work accordingly. The same time delay applies to special finishes or any changes you make to the original plans.

Opposite: *There's a hint of times gone by in this new cottage-style kitchen thanks to old-fashioned features, such as beadboard wood cabinetry, nostalgic light fixtures, and the vintage pattern of the floor tile. The cabinets, which were custom made, took 8 weeks to deliver.*

SMART STEPS

ONE *Preplanning*

- Make the decision to remodel
- Assess the problems and goals involved
- Gather ideas, and review trends
- Develop a budget, and obtain financing
- Collect information about contractors
- Arrange interviews with contractors
- Select a contractor

THREE *Design & Agreement*

- Presentation of preliminary drawings and project specifications
- Review and discuss options
- Sign a design agreement

4 weeks	1 week	2-3 weeks	2-4 weeks

TWO *Initial Meetings*

- Walk-through of the existing space
- Brainstorm with the contractor
- Decide whether the project is feasible within the budget
- Sign a letter of intent if you're purchasing design services, or skip to step 4

FOUR *Design Development/Preconstruction*

- Review completed drawings and project notes
- Clarify any misunderstandings about the scope and intent of the project
- Select products
- Sign the construction contract
- Make the first downpayment
- Wait three days for the Right of Recision period to pass, if applicable
- Obtain permits
- Meet with the construction team, and sign a preconstruction agreement

161

FIVE *After Permits Are Issued*

- 🐛 Order products
- 🐛 Finalize the project schedule, and distribute it
- 🐛 Discuss impact of project on home life with the family, including safety and keeping pets out of the workplace
- 🐛 Remove personal items and breakables from the construction area

SEVEN *The Final Stages*

- 🐛 Inspect the job, and establish list of final details to make sure everything is completed to your satisfaction
- 🐛 Obtain the final inspection and certificate of occupancy or habitability
- 🐛 Make a substantial completion payment

| 1 week | 4-8 weeks | 1 week | 1 week |

SIX *The Work*

- 🐛 Complete the demolition
- 🐛 Complete the framing
- 🐛 Rough-in mechanical systems
- 🐛 Install the drywall
- 🐛 Install the flooring
- 🐛 Install the cabinetry
- 🐛 Install fixtures
- 🐛 Do the finishing work (painting and wallpapering)

EIGHT *The Conclusion*

- 🐛 Give the final approval
- 🐛 Make the final payment

CONCLUSION

A well-designed new kitchen will improve the way you live in and enjoy your home. It will transform everyday tasks and commonplace chores, turning them into social occasions or shared activities with family and friends.

To make your new kitchen everything you want it to be, it's important to learn as much as you can about the process of design and the products and materials that will ultimately fill up the space and do a lot of the work—before you embark on the actual physical job. Education is your key to success. As you go along, be open to innovative ideas; don't be afraid to try new things on paper. But don't get in over your head. When you need help, ask for it. Professional assistance can make the difference between disaster and perfection.

Although seeing the project through from beginning to end isn't easy, you'll forget all about the sawdust and the hammering, and the days when you wondered why you ever got involved in such an enormous undertaking, when you finally sit down for your first cup of coffee in the new kitchen. Until then, keep your eye on the goal and know that you are taking part in a creative adventure that will add value to your home and quality to the time spent there. Hopefully, *The Smart Approach to Kitchen Design* has provided the inspiration to get you started. ❧

Opposite: *By making this kitchen more efficient and sociable, the owners have created an environment that enhances the pleasure of a good meal in the company of friends and family.*

APPENDIX: KITCHEN TEMPLATES

Cabinets

6"x24"	6"x24"	6"x24"	6"x24"	6"x24"	6"x24"	desk 36"x24"	desk 30"x24"	9"x24"	9"x24"	9"x24"	9"x24"	9"x24"	9"x24"	9"x24"	9"x24"	

12"x24"	12"x24"	12"x24"	12"x24"	12"x24"	12"x24"	12"x24"	6"x24"	base cabinet 15"x24"	base cabinet 15"x24"	base cabinet 15"x24"	base cabinet 15"x24"	base cabinet 15"x24"	base cabinet 15"x24"	base cabinet 15"x24"	base cabinet 15"x24"

base cabinet 15"x24"	9"x24"	6"x24"	base cabinet 18"x24"	base cabinet 18"x24"	base cabinet 18"x24"	base cabinet 18"x24"	base cabinet 18"x24"	base cabinet 18"x24"	base cabinet 18"x24"	base cabinet 18"x24"	base cabinet 18"x24"	base cabinet 18"x24"	base cabinet 18"x24"

base cabinet 21"x24"	base cabinet 21"x24"	base cabinet 21"x24"	base cabinet 21"x24"	base cabinet 21"x24"	base cabinet 21"x24"	9"x24"	base cabinet 24"x24"	base cabinet 24"x24"	base cabinet 24"x24"	base cabinet 24"x24"	base cabinet 24"x24"

base cabinet 24"x24"	base cabinet 24"x24"	base cabinet 24"x24"	base cabinet 24"x24"	base cabinet 24"x24"	9"x24"	base cabinet 27"x24"	base cabinet 27"x24"	base cabinet 27"x24"	base cabinet 27"x24"	base cabinet 27"x24"

base cabinet 27"x24"	base cabinet 15"x24"	base cabinet 30"x24"	base cabinet 30"x24"	base cabinet 30"x24"	base cabinet 30"x24"	base cabinet 30"x24"	base cabinet 30"x24"	base cabinet 30"x24"	base cabinet 30"x24"

base cabinet 33"x24"	base cabinet 33"x24"	base cabinet 33"x24"	base cabinet 33"x24"	base cabinet 33"x24"	12"x24"	base cabinet 36"x24"	base cabinet 36"x24"	base cabinet 36"x24"

base cabinet 36"x24"	base cabinet 36"x24"	base cabinet 36"x24"	base cabinet 36"x24"	base cabinet 36"x24"	base cabinet 36"x24"	base cabinet 39"x24"	base cabinet 39"x24"

base cabinet 39"x24"	base cabinet 39"x24"	base cabinet 39"x24"	base cabinet 42"x24"	base cabinet 42"x24"	base cabinet 42"x24"	base cabinet 18"x24"	base cabinet 18"x24"

base cabinet 42"x24"	base cabinet 45"x24"	base cabinet 45"x24"	base cabinet 45"x24"	base cabinet 45"x24"	base cabinet 45"x24"	base cabinet 45"x24"

base cabinet 45"x24"	left-hand corner-base cabinet 36"x24"	left-hand corner-base cabinet 36"x24"	left-hand corner-base cabinet 36"x24"	right-hand corner-base cabinet 36"x24"	right-hand corner-base cabinet 36"x24"	right-hand corner-base cabinet 36"x24"	right-hand corner-base cabinet 36"x24"

Pantry Cabinets

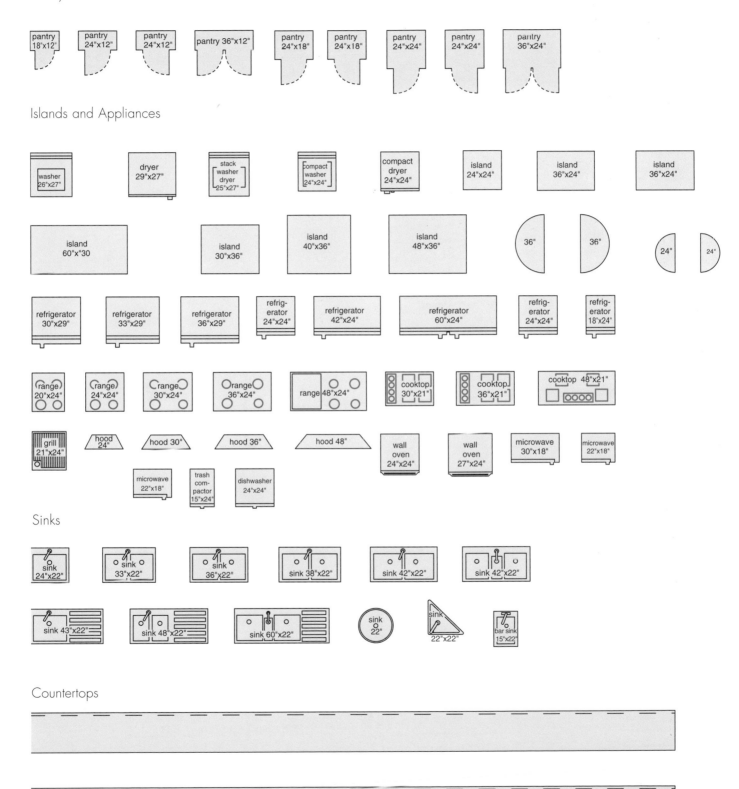

pantry 18"x12" pantry 24"x12" pantry 24"x12" pantry 36"x12" pantry 24"x18" pantry 24"x18" pantry 24"x24" pantry 24"x24" pantry 36"x24"

Islands and Appliances

washer 26"x27" dryer 29"x27" stack washer dryer 25"x27" compact washer 24"x24" compact dryer 24"x24" island 24"x24" island 36"x24" island 36"x24"

island 60"x"30 island 30"x36" island 40"x36" island 48"x36" 36" 36" 24" 24"

refrigerator 30"x29" refrigerator 33"x29" refrigerator 36"x29" refrigerator 24"x24" refrigerator 42"x24" refrigerator 60"x24" refrigerator 24"x24" refrigerator 18'x24"

range 20"x24" range 24"x24" range 30"x24" range 36"x24" range 48"x24" cooktop 30"x21" cooktop 36"x21" cooktop 48"x21"

grill 21"x24" hood 24" hood 30" hood 36" hood 48" wall oven 24"x24" wall oven 27"x24" microwave 30"x18" microwave 22"x18"

microwave 22"x18" trash compactor 15"x24" dishwasher 24"x24"

Sinks

sink 24"x22" sink 33"x22" sink 36"x22" sink 38"x22" sink 42"x22" sink 42"x22"

sink 43"x22" sink 48"x22" sink 60"x22" sink 22" sink 22"x22" bar sink 15"x22"

Countertops

Windows

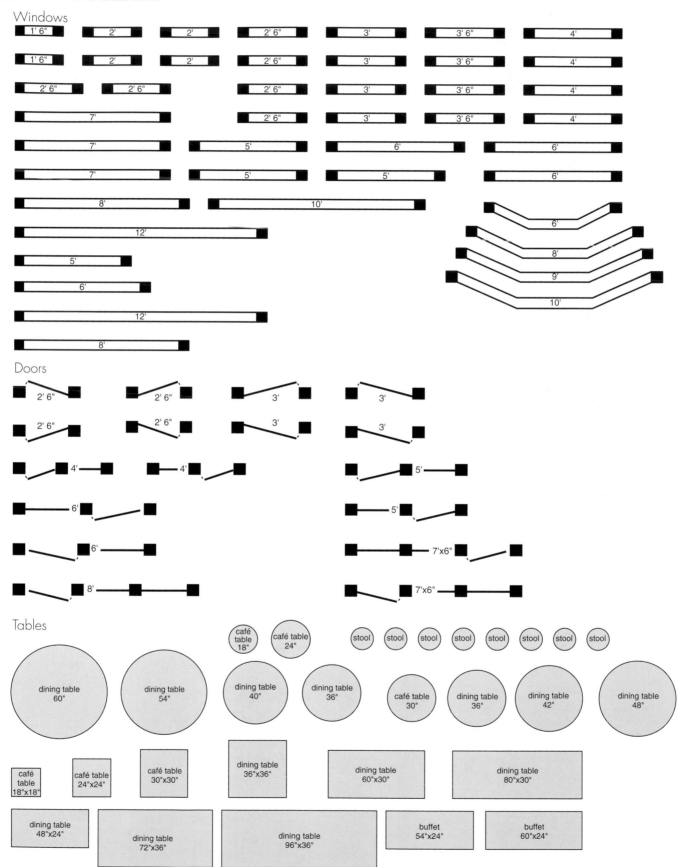

Doors

Tables

Scale: 1 square = 1 foot

GLOSSARY

OF KITCHEN TERMS

Absorption (light): The light energy (wavelengths) not reflected by an object or substance. The color of a substance depends on the wavelength reflected.

Accent Light: A type of light that highlights an area to emphasize that aspect of a room's character.

Accessible Designs: Those that accommodate persons with physical disabilities.

Adaptable Designs: Those that can be easily changed to accommodate a person with disabilities.

Ambient Light: General light that surrounds a room and is not focused.

Antiscalding Valve (Pressure-Balancing Valve): A fitting that contains a piston that automatically responds to changes in line water pressure to maintain temperature; the valve blocks abrupt drops or rises in temperature.

Awning Window: A window that is hinged at the top and swings outward when open.

Backlighting: Illumination coming from a source behind or at the side of an object.

Backsplash: The vertical part at the rear and sides of a countertop that protects the adjacent wall.

Barrier-Free Fixture: A fixture specifically designed for people who use wheelchairs or who have limited mobility.

Base Cabinet: A cabinet that rests on the floor and supports a countertop.

Base Plan: A map of the existing kitchen that shows detailed measurements and the location of cabinets, appliances, sinks, and any fixed elements.

Basin: A shallow sink.

Bump Out: Living space created by cantilevering the floor and ceiling joists and extending the exterior wall of a room.

Butcher Block: A countertop material composed of strips of hardwood laminated together and sealed against moisture penetration.

Candlepower (Cp): The intensity of light measured at a lamp. This term is generally used for task and accent lighting.

Cantilever: A structural beam supported on one end. A cantilever can be used to support a small addition.

Casement Window: A window that consists of one or two framed-glass panels that are hinged on the side and swing outward at the turn of a crank.

Centerline: The bisecting line through the center of an object, such as a sink.

cfm: An abbreviation that refers to cubic feet of air that is moved per minute by an exhaust fan.

Clearance: The amount of space between two fixtures, the centerlines of two fixtures, or a fixture and an obstacle, such as a wall. Clearances may be mandated by codes.

Code: A locally or nationally enforced mandate regarding structural design, materials, plumbing, or electrical systems that state what you can or cannot do when you build or remodel. Codes are intended to protect standards of health, safety, and land use.

Color Intensity: Strength of a color.

Color Rendition Index (CRI): Measures the way a light source renders color. The higher the number, the more the color resembles how it appears in sunlight.

Contemporary Style: A style of decoration or architecture that is modern and pertains to what is current.

Correlated Color Temperature (CCT): Compares the apparent warmth or coolness of discontinuous-spectrum light.

Fittings: The plumbing devices that bring water to the fixtures. These can include faucets, spouts, and drains, etc.

Fixed Window: A window that cannot be opened. It is usually a decorative unit, such as a half-round or Palladian-style window.

Fixture: Any fixed part of the structural design, such as sinks, windows, or doors.

Fixture Spacing: Refers to how far apart to space ambient-light fixtures for an even field of light.

Fluorescent Light Bulb: An energy-efficient light source made of a usually tubular-shaped bulb that contains a glowing gas and is coated on the inside with phosporous.

Foot-Candle (Fc): A unit used to measure the brightness produced by a lamp. A foot-candle is equal to one lumen per square foot of surface.

Framed Cabinet: A cabinet with a full frame across the face of the cabinet box.

Frameless Cabinet: A cabinet without a face frame. It may also be called a "European-style" cabinet.

Ground-Fault Circuit Interrupter (GFCI): A safety circuit breaker that compares the amount of current entering a receptacle with the amount leaving. If there is a discrepancy of 0.005 volt, the GFCI breaks the circuit in a fraction of a second. GFCIs are required by the National Electrical Code in areas of the house that are subject to dampness.

Grout: A binder and filler applied to the joints between ceramic tile.

Halogen Light Bulb: A bulb that uses metal halides to provide incandescent light that is whiter and brighter than standard incandescent lamps.

Highlight: The lightest tone in a room.

Incandescent Light: A bulb that contains a conductive wire filament through which current flows. This is the most common type of light source.

Load-Bearing Wall: A wall that supports part of a structure's weight. Openings in any load-bearing wall must be reinforced to carry the live and dead loads of the structure's weight.

Lumen: A term that refers to the intensity of light measured at a light source that is used for general or ambient lighting.

Muntins: Framing members of a window that divide the panes of glass.

Palette: A range of colors that complement each other in a scheme.

Peninsula: A countertop, with or without a base cabinet, that is connected at one end to a wall or another counter and extends outward, providing access on three sides.

Pressure-Balancing Valve See "Antiscalding Valve."

Skylight: A framed opening in the roof that admits sunlight into the house. It can be covered with either a flat glass panel or plastic dome.

Snap-In Grilles: Ready-made rectangular or diamond-pattern grilles that snap into a window sash and create the look of a true divided-light window.

Soffit: The area just below the ceiling and above the wall cabinets. It may be boxed in or open.

Space Reconfiguration: A term used to describe the reallocation of interior space without adding on.

Spout: The projecting tube-like orifice from which water flows out of a faucet.

Subfloor: The material applied directly to the floor joists on top of which the finished floor rests.

Task Lighting: Lighting designed to illuminate a particular task area.

Reflectance Levels: The amount of light that is reflected from a colored surface, such as a tile wall or painted surface.

Roof Window: A window that is installed on the roof and can be opened to provide ventilation.

Schematic: A detailed diagram of systems (such as plumbing or electrical) within a home.

Sight Line: The natural line of sight the eye travels when looking into or around a room.

Tone: Degree of lightness or darkness of a color.

Universal Design: Products and room designs that are easy to use by people of all ages and varying abilities.

Wall Cabinet: A cabinet, usually 12 inches deep, that's mounted on the wall a minimum of 12 inches above a countertop.

Work Triangle: The area bounded by the lines that connect the sink, range, and refrigerator.

INDEX

PHOTO CREDITS

Cover: *Photographer: Nancy Hill.* **Introduction:** *Courtesy of Jenn-Air.* **p. 1** *Photographer: Philip Clayton-Thompson.* **p. 2** *Photographer: Brian Vanden Brink.* **p. 6** *Photographer: Mark Samu.* **p. 10–11** *Photographer: David Duncan Livingston.com.* **p. 12–13** *Photographer: (right, below & opposite): David Duncan Livingston.com.* **p. 14** *Photographer: David Duncan Livingston.com.* **p. 15–17** *Photographer: John Schwartz; Designer: Alan Asarnow, CKD, CBD, CR for Ulrich, Inc.* **p. 19** *Photographer: Duncan David Livingston.com.* **p. 20–21** *Photographer: (above & opposite): Alan Shortall.* **p. 22–23** *Photographer: John Schwartz; Designer: Stephan Kinon, CKD for Ulrich, Inc.* **p. 24–25** *Photographer: (right & opposite): Andrew McKinney; Designer: Lu Ann Bauer.* **p. 26–27** *Photographer: Andrew McKinney; Designer: Lu Ann Bauer.* **p. 28–30** *Photographer: Alan Shortall.* **p. 31** *Photographer: John Schwartz; Designer: Sharon L. Sherman, CKD for Ulrich, Inc.* **p. 32** *Photographer: David Duncan Livingston.com.* **p. 33** *Photographer: Mark Samu, Reprinted with permission from House Beautiful Kitchen/Baths © 1997, The Hearst Corporation; Designer: Eileen Boyd Interiors.* **p. 34** *Photographer: Jessie Walker.* **p. 35–36** *Photographer: Mark Samu.* **p. 39** *Photographer: Mark Samu.* **p. 42** *Photographer: Melabee M Miller; Designer: Steven Meltzer & Karen S. Khalaf, AIA.* **p. 48** *Photographer: David Duncan Livingston.com.* **p. 48–49** *Photographer: Melabee M Miller.* **p. 50–51** *Photographer: Tria Giovan.* **p. 52–53** *Photographer: Grey Crawford.* **p. 54** *Photographer: Jessie Walker.* **p. 55** *Photographer: Nancy Hill.* **p. 56–57** *Courtesy of KraftMaid Cabinetry.* **p. 59** *Photographer: Gary McKinstry, Courtesy of the National Kitchen & Bath Association; Designer: Donna L. A. Riddell, CKD, CBD.* **p. 60–61** *Photographer: Andrew McKinney; Designer: Lu Ann Bauer.* **p. 62** *Photographer: Mark Samu.* **p. 63** *Courtesy of Heritage Custom Cabinetry.* **p. 64**

Photographer: Philip Clayton-Thompson. **p. 65** *Photographer: Nancy Hill.* **p. 66** *Photographer: Tria Giovan.* **p. 67** *Photographer: Philip Clayton-Thompson.* **p. 68** *Photographer: (clockwise): David Duncan Livingston.com. Photographer: Mark Samu. Photographer: Jessie Walker.* **p. 70** *Photographer: Mark Samu.* **p. 71** *Photographer: (left): Melabee M Miller; Designer: Linda Daly, ASID. Photographer: (below): David Duncan Livingston.com.* **p. 72** *Photographer: Nancy Hill.* **p. 74** *Photographer: David Duncan Livingston. com.* **p. 75** *Photographer: John Schwartz; Designer: Sharon L. Sherman, CKD for Ulrich, Inc.* **p. 76** *Photographer: David Duncan Living-ston.com.* **p. 77** *Photographer: Nancy Hill.* **p. 78** *Photographer: David Duncan Living-ston.com.* **p. 79** *Photographer: Mark Samu, Reprinted with permission from House Beautiful Kitchen/Baths © 1998, The Hearst Corporation. Styling by Margaret Mc-Nicholas; Designer: Peter Cook A.I.A.* **p. 80** *Photographer: Mark Samu.* **p. 81** *Photographer: David Duncan Livingston. com.* **p. 82–83** *Photographer: Mark Samu.* **p. 84–85** *Photographer: John Schwartz.* **p. 86–87** *Photographer: David Duncan Livingston.com.* **p. 88** *Photographer: (top & bottom): Mark Samu Reprinted with permission from House Beautiful Kitchen/Baths © 1997, The Hearst Corporation. Styling by Margaret McNicholas; Designer: Shaver Melahn Studios.* **p. 89** *Photographer: (above left): David Duncan Livingston.com. Photographer: (above & left): Nancy Hill.* **p. 90** *Photographer: (above & below): Andrew McKinney; Designer: Lu Ann Bauer.* **p. 91** *Photographer: Andrew McKinney; Designer: Lu Ann Bauer.* **p. 92** *Photographer: (left & above): Nancy Hill; Designer: Mary Fisher Designs.* **p. 93** *Photographer: (left): Grey Crawford. Photographer: (right): Mark Samu, Reprinted with permission from House Beautiful Kitchen/Baths © 1997, The Hearst Corporation. Styling by Margaret McNicholas; Designer: Shaver*

Melahn Studios. **p. 94** *Photographer: (bottom left): David Duncan Livingston.com. Photographer: (bottom right): Tria Giovan.* **p. 95** *Photographer: (left): Nancy Hill. Photographer: (right): Brian Vanden Brink.* **p. 96–98** *Photographer: John Schwartz.* **p. 99** *Photographer: David Duncan Livingston.com.* **p. 100** *Photographer: Mark Samu.* **p. 101–102** *Photographer: Tria Giovan.* **p. 103** *Photographer: Mark Samu.* **p. 104** *Photographer: Andrew Mc Kinney; Designer: Lu Ann Bauer.* **p. 105** *Photographer: David Duncan Livingston. com.* **p. 106** *Photographer: Mark Samu, Reprinted with permission from House Beautiful Kitchen/ Baths © 1998, The Hearst Corporation. Styling by Margaret McNicholas.* **p. 107** *Photographer: Mark Samu.* **p. 108** *Photographer: Nancy Hill.* **p. 109** *Photographer: Melabee M Miller; Designer: Ellen Brounstein.* **p. 110–111** *Photographer: Nancy Hill.* **p. 112** *Courtesy of Sub-zero.* **p. 113** *Courtesy of GE.* **p. 114** *Photographer: (left & below): David Duncan Livingston .com.* **p. 115–116** *Photographer: David Duncan Livingston.com.* **p. 118–119** *Photographer: Philip Clayton-Thompson; Designer: Mary Kaiser, Ltd.* **p. 120** *Photographer: John Schwartz; Designer: Tess Giuliani, CKD for Ulrich, Inc.* **p. 122–124** *Photographer: Mark Samu; Designer: Montllor Box A.I.A.* **p. 125** *Photographer: David Duncan Livingston. com.* **p. 126** *Photographer: Mark Samu; Designer: EJR Architects.* **p. 128** *Photographer: Andrew McKinney; Designer: Lu Ann Bauer.* **p. 129** *Photographer: Mark Samu, Re-printed with permission from House Beautiful Kitchen/ Baths © 1997, The Hearst Corporation. Styling by Margaret McNicholas.* **p. 130** *Photographer: Mark Samu, Re-printed with permission from House Beautiful Kitchen/ Baths © 1998, The Hearst Corporation. Styling by Margaret McNicholas; Designer: Peter Cook A.I.A.* **p. 132** *Photographer: Melabee M Miller; Designer: Ellen Brounstein.* **p. 133** *Photographer: Mark Samu; Designer: EJR Architects*

p. 135 *Photographer: Mark Samu.* **p. 136–139** *Photographer: Andrew McKinney, Designer: Lu Ann Bauer.* **p. 140–141** *Photographer: Mark Samu, Reprinted with permission from House Beautiful Kitchen/Baths © 1997, The Hearst Corporation; Designer: Eileen Boyd Interiors.* **p. 142–143** *Photographer: David Duncan Livingston.com.* **p. 144–145** *Photographer: Nancy Hill.* **p. 146** *Photographer: (left & right): Tria Giovan.* **p. 147** *Photographer: Tria Giovan.* **p. 148–149** *Photographer: Francis Hammond.* **p. 150** *Photographer: David Duncan Livingston.com.* **p. 151** *Photographer: David Duncan Livingston.com; Designer: Cooper Kitchens.* **p. 152–153** *Photographer: Holly Stickley.* **p. 154–155** *Photographer: Mark Samu, Reprinted with permission from House Beautiful Kitchen/ Baths © 1998, The Hearst Corporation. Styling by Margaret McNicholas; Designer: Lucianna Samu.* **p. 156** *Photographer: Mark Samu, Reprinted with permission from House Beautiful Kitchen/ Baths © 1998, The Hearst Corporation. Styling by Margaret McNicholas; Designer: Lucianna Samu.* **p. 157** *Photographer: Philip Clayton-Thompson.* **p. 158–159** *Photo courtesy of Wood-Mode Cabinetry.* **p. 160** *Photographer: (top left): Mark Samu; Designer: Rechlar Kitchen. Photographer: (bottom left): Mark Samu.* **p. 160–161** *Photographer: Mark Samu; Designer: Rechlar Kitchen.* **p. 161** *Photographer: (clockwise top to middle left): Mark Samu; Designer: Edwards Kitchen. Photographer: Mark Samu; Designer: Edwards Kitchen. Photographer: Mark Samu. Photographer: Mark Samu; Designer: Edwards Kitchen. Photographer: Mark Samu.* **p. 162** *Photographer: Mark Samu.* **p. 168–169** *Photographer: Melabee M Miller.* **Back Cover:** *Photographer: (Clockwise from top to left): Tria Giovan. Photographer: Alan Shortall. Photographer: David Duncan Livingston.com.*

SOURCES

Photographers
Brian Vanden Brink, Rockport, ME; 207/236-4035. **Grey Crawford,** Los Angeles, CA; 213/413-4299. **Mark Darley,** San Francisco, CA; 415/381-5452. **Tria Giovan,** New York, NY; 212/533-6612. **Francis Hammond,** New York, NY; 212/242-7519. **Nancy Hill,** Ridge Field, CT; 203/431-7655. **David Duncan Livingston,** Mill Valley, CA; 415/383-0898. **Andrew McKinney,** San Francisco, CA; 415/752-4070. **Melabee M Miller,** Hillside, NJ; 908/527-0242. **Mark Samu,** Bayport, NY; 212/754-0415. **John Schwartz,** New York, NY; 212/567-9727. **Alan Shortall,** Chicago, IL; 773/252-3747.

Holly Stickley, Tigard, OR; 503/639-4278. **Philip Clayton-Thompson,** Portland, OR; 503/234-4883. **Jessie Walker,** Glencoe, IL; 847/835-0522.

Designers, Artists, and Architects
Alan Asarnaw, CKD, CBD, CR, **Ulrich, Inc.,** Ridgewood, NJ; 201/445-1260. **Lu Ann Bauer,** San Francisco, CA; 415/621-7262. **Eileen Boyd Interiors,** Huntington, NY; 516/427-6400. **Ellen Brounstein,** Brown-stone Interiors, Summit, NJ; 908/277-6715. **Peter Cook** A.I.A., Southhampton, NY; 516/283-0077. **Cooper Kitchens,** Santa Rosa, CA; 707/542-7669. **Bruce Curtis and Sue Balk,** Washtenaw Woodwrights, Ann Arbor, MI; 313/994-8797. **Linda Daly,**

ASID, Ivyland, PA; 515/598-3345. **EJR Architects,** Oyster Bay Cove, NY; 516/922-2479. **Mary Fisher Designs,** Scottsdale, AZ; 480/473-0986. **Tess Giuliani,** CKD, and **Stephen Finon,** CKD, **Ulrich Inc.,** Ridgewood, NJ; 201/445-1260. **Karen S. Khalaf,** AIA, Summit, NJ; 908/273-3233. **Mary Kaiser,** Ltd., Port Townsend, WA; 800/831-7483. **Steven Meltzer, Abby Kitchens & Baths,** Millburn, NJ; 973/763-6223. **Montl-lor Box** A.I.A., Port Washington, NY; 516/883-7719. **Donna L.A. Riddell,** CKD, CBD, Victoria B.C. **Lucianna Samu,** Blue Point, NY; 516/363-5902. **Shaver Melahn Studios,** New York, NY; 212/366-9783. **Ulrich, Inc.,** Ridgewood, NJ; 201/445-1260.

Manufacturers and Associations-General Electric Company; Louisville, KY; 800/626-2000. **Heritage Custom Kitchens,** New Holland, PA; 717/354-4011. **KraftMaid Cabinetry,** Passport Series, Cleveland, OH; 800/571-1990. **The Jenn-Air Company,** Blue Creek Collection, Indianapolis, IN; 800/536-6247. **National Association of the Remodeling Industry** (NARI), Alexandria, VA; 800/966-7601. **National Kitchen & Bath Association (NKBA),** Hackettstown, NJ; 800/401-NKBA. **Sub-Zero Freezer Co., Inc.,** Madison, WI; 800/222-7820. **Wood-Mode Cabinetry,** Kreamer, PA; 717/374-2711.

Have a home decorating, improvement, or gardening project? Look for these and other fine **Creative Homeowner books** wherever books are sold. . .

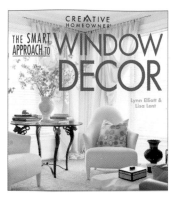

Design advice and industry tips for choosing window treatments. Over 225 illustrations. 176pp.; 9"×10"
BOOK # 279431

How to work with space, color, pattern, texture. Over 300 photos. 256 pp.; 9"×10"
BOOK #: 279667

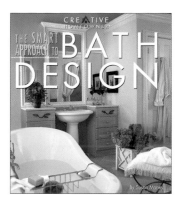

All you need to know about designing a bath. Over 150 color photos. 176 pp.; 9"×10"
BOOK #: 287225

Master stenciling, sponging, glazing, marbling, and more. Over 300 illustrations. 272 pp.; 9"×10"
BOOK #: 279550

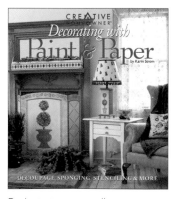

Projects to personalize your rooms with paint and paper. 300 color photos. 176 pp.; 9"×10"
BOOK #: 279723

Learn how to make the most of color. More than 150 color photos. 176 pp.; 9"×10"
BOOK #: 287264

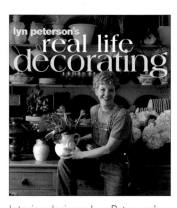

Interior designer Lyn Peterson's easy-to-live-with decorating ideas. Over 350 photos. 304 pp.; 9"×10"
BOOK #: 279382

Advice for choosing tile for interior and exterior decorating projects. Over 250 photos. 176 pp.; 9"×10"
BOOK #: 279824

Complete houseplant guide. 200 readily available plants; more than 400 photos. 192 pp.; 9"×10"
BOOK #: 275243

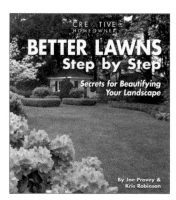

Create beautiful, healthier, lower-maintenance lawns. Over 300 illustrations. 160 pp.; 9"×10"
BOOK #: 274359

Complete DIY tile instruction. Over 350 color photos and illustration. 160 pp.; 8¹/₂"×10⁷/₈"
BOOK #: 277524

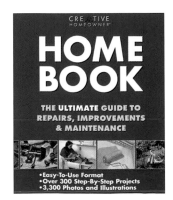

The ultimate home-improvement reference manual. 300+ step-by-step projects. 608 pp.; 9"×10⁷/₈"
BOOK #: 267855

For more information, and to order direct, call 800-631-7795; in New Jersey 201-934-7100.
Please visit our Web site at www.creativehomeowner.com